SCHOLASTIC $12

W9-BZB-397

Ingredients

MELVILLE SENIOR HIGH SCHOOL
188119.01
LIBRARY

641.5622 MCC
4 ingredients : kids
McCosker, Kim
Copy No: 1 BookID: 188119.01
340340413662

4
Ingredients
KIDS

4 Ingredients
PO Box 400
Caloundra QLD 4551

ABN: 19 307 118 068

www.4ingredients.com.au
info@4ingredients.com.au

4 Ingredients Kids

Copyright © Meymott Enterprises Pty Ltd and PR International Pty Ltd

Published by 4 Ingredients 2011

The moral right of the authors has been asserted.

All rights reserved. Without limiting the rights under copyright reserved above, no part of this publication may be reproduced, stored in or introduced into a retrieval system, or transmitted, in any form or by any means (electronic, mechanical, photocopying, recording, or otherwise), without the prior written permission of the authors and the publisher of this book.

Cover & Formatting: Tara Hale Illustration and Design, www.tarahale.com
Printing & Binding: Griffin Press, Australia

UK Publisher:	Simon & Schuster (020) 7316 1900
AUS Distributor:	Simon & Schuster +61 2 9983 6600
NZ Distributor:	Random House +64 9 444 7197
USA Publisher:	Atria Books (a division of Simon & Schuster) 212/698-7172

ISBN: 978-0-9806294-1-5

Foreword

Welcome to the most requested cookbook in our *4 Ingredients* cookbook series; *4 Ingredients Kids*!

Ever since we wrote our very first *4 Ingredients* book back in 2007, we've both been super keen to write a kids cookbook. When we commenced our *4 Ingredients* journey together, we had 3 little boys between us. Over the past 4 years we've had 3 more — ALL boys can you believe??!!!!??

Our love, passion and desire to feed and nurture our 6 beautiful little boys is what instigated *4 Ingredients* to become a reality. Educating them through the discovery of taste and textures has not only eliminated the meal-time tantrums (most of the time ☺), it's developed a healthy love of food and taught them a new life skill — cooking!

We have travelled millions of miles in the search for sensational new recipes that will delight even the fussiest of eaters. We have cooked hundreds of recipes that have all been 'taste tested' by a panel of 6 mini experts who we would like to thank; Morgan, Jaxson, Hamilton, Flynn, Bowie and Casey.

We have loved cooking and creating hundreds of delicious recipes for babies, toddlers, teenagers (and us BIG kids) to bring you *4 Ingredients Kids*. As a result, it is very dear to our hearts and we hope you'll have as much fun using it as we did creating it.

Thank you also to the Melinda Dines, Jeannette McCosker, Cathy Bennett, Michelle Tuite, Michelle Evans, Joy Duke, Janelle McCosker, Angie Corvino, Kate Guiver and Glen Turnbull for all your help in and out of the kitchen. You are all beautiful parents and friends.

We'd like to dedicate this book to every Mum, Dad, Grandma, Grandpa and carer who strives and delights in feeding kids home-cooked meals lovingly prepared. We hope some of these become family favourites that your kids can pass onto their kids too!

Happy Cooking!

Rachael & Kim

Letter from a Parent

This was submitted by Jennifer Houston, July 2010.

To Jenny and the many like her asking for such a book …
This one's for you!

Hi!

I was just wondering what your plans are for the next book? (I assume there will be one?) Have you thought about targetting the kids market?

I have two boys very VERY interested in cooking, and I love your first two books (don't have the gluten free one) and I would love a book that was directed at kids, with the simplicity of your 4 ingredient recipes.

I know as an ex-teacher I would have used it in the classroom too. Just a thought … I would love to know if you were interested in the idea …

Thanks for your time.

Jenny

Kitchen Alphabet

There are many benefits to involving kids in the kitchen; they learn to start and finish a task, learning to cook is an invaluable life skill and it can help with their basic maths and spelling skills …

Teach your kids the alphabet in a fun and engaging way using the everyday products in your kitchen.

Here's our Kitchen Alphabet … What's yours?

A	—	Apples
B	—	Bananas
C	—	Caramel
D	—	Delicious
E	—	Egg
F	—	Fruit Salad
G	—	Grapes
H	—	Hamburgers
I	—	Ice-cream
J	—	Jelly
K	—	Kebab
L	—	Lemon
M	—	Mandarin
N	—	Nutella
O	—	Orange
P	—	Pizza
Q	—	Quiche
R	—	Raspberry
S	—	Spaghetti
T	—	Tomato Sauce
U	—	Udon Noodles
V	—	Vegemite
W	—	Watermelon
X	—	Xmas Cake
Y	—	Yoghurt
Z	—	Zest

Table of Contents

In the Cupboard

4 Ingredients offers a wide range of yummy recipes, cooked for our families and friends for many a BBQ, party, Sunday dinner, Friday nibbles and so on. In all our trials and errors there seemed to be a bunch of staple ingredients we always called upon. What we aim to do in this section is help you stock your kitchen pantry with those basic ingredients that will help flavour, make and save many a dish and event from peril.

Please note: In this book we have not included salt, pepper and water as part of the 4 Ingredients.

SAVOURY	SWEET
Basil Pesto	Arrowroot biscuits
BBQ sauce	Caster sugar
Beef and chicken stock cubes	Cinnamon
Bread crumbs	Condensed milk
Brown rice	Cornflour
Cold pressed extra virgin macadamia oil	Cream cheese
Dijon mustard	Eggs
Extra virgin macadamia oil spray	Evaporated milk
French onion soup (dry mix)	Food colouring
Fresh garlic	Gelatine
Garlic powder	Honey
Jasmine rice	Icing sugar
Lemons	Jams: apricot, strawberry
Minced ginger	Jelly crystals
Peppercorns	Marmalade
Pine nuts	Mixed fruit
Sea salt	Mixed spices
Sesame seeds and oil	Nutmeg
Sour cream	Packet of bamboo skewers
Soy sauce	Plain flour
Spaghetti and Noodles	Puff pastry
Sweet-chilli sauce	Rapadura sugar
Tinned soups: mushroom, chicken tomato, asparagus	Self raising flour
Tomato sauce	Tin of crushed pineapple
Vinegar	Vanilla essence
Whole-egg mayonnaise	Yoghurt
Wholegrain mustard	
Worcestershire sauce	

Guide to Weights & Measures

To help a recipe turn out right, you need to measure right. To make is easier for all of you budding cooks, a big fancy conversion table is not required, all you need to make the recipes within 4 Ingredients are:

1 teaspoon: 1 tsp.

1 tablespoon: 1 tbs.

1 cup: 250ml

or the following:

Product	Grams per Cup	Product	Grams per Cup
Almond meal	170	Nuts – Pistachios	120
BBQ sauce	280	Nuts – Walnuts	100
Butter	230	Pasta (dried)	75
Basil Pesto	260	Pasta sauce	175
Breadcrumbs	130	Peanut butter	260
Cheese	100	Popcorn	40
Chutney	300	Polenta	100
Cornflakes	120	Raisins	170
Cornflour	120	Rice	185
Desiccated coconut	120	Rice bubbles	80
Dried apricots	160	Rolled oats	100
Dried mixed fruit	170	Salsa	175
Flour – Plain	175	Sour cream	320
Flour – Self Raising	175	Sultanas	170
Honey	320	Sugar – Brown	220
Icing sugar	120	Sugar – Caster	200
Jam	320	Sugar – Raw	200
Maple syrup	240	Sugar – White	220
Mayonnaise	260	Sweet chilli sauce	320
Natural muesli	110	Tandoori paste	225
Nuts – Almonds	160	Tomato paste	260
Nuts – Pecans	120	Tomato sauce	280
Nuts – Pine nuts	160	Yoghurt	250

Hint: When you measure dry ingredients like flour and sugar, always hold the measuring cup over the container of flour or sugar while you fill it up.

Abbreviations Used

Gram	g
Kilogram	kg
Millilitre	ml
Litre	ltr

Oven Temperature Guide

Making friends with your oven really helps when cooking. Basically the Celsius temperature is about half the Fahrenheit temperature.

A lot of ovens these days offer the option to bake or fan bake (amongst others), as a rule, having the fan assisted option on will greatly increase the temperature in your oven and will shorten cooking times.

Our recipes have been compiled assuming a static conventional oven (non fan-forced) unless otherwise stated. If however your oven is fan forced, as a general rule of thumb, conventional cooking temperatures are reduced by 20°C (this may vary between models). So if the recipe reads bake for 1 hour at 200°C that will be 1 hour at 180°C fan-forced.

Here's some help:

	Slow	Slow	Mod	Mod	Mod hot	Mod hot	Hot	Hot	Very hot
Fahrenheit	275	300	325	350	375	400	425	450	475
Celsius	140	150	165	180	190	200	220	230	240
Gas Mark	1	2	3	4	5	6	7	8	9

Cooking Made Easy

Al dente: Often found in pasta recipes. It means to cook the pasta just until it's done, not soft or overcooked.

Au gratin: Refers to a baked dish, such as a casserole, topped with cheese or breadcrumbs, then browned on top, either in the oven or under a broiler.

Baste: Spooning or brushing food with a liquid — such as butter, broth, or the cooking liquid — to help the food stay moist during cooking.

Blanch: Placing food briefly in boiling water and then plunging into cold water to halt cooking. Blanching loosens the skins of fruits and vegetables to help peel them more easily.

Boil: The boiling process serves two purposes; it destroys organic impurities, and it transforms raw ingredients into cooked foods. Interestingly, boiling water is affected by altitude, the higher you climb the lower the boiling point. Water boils at sea level at 212°F or 100°C.

Braise: Slowly cooking browned foods in a small amount of liquid in a tightly covered pot.

Brown: To brown a meat means to cook until brown. You may brown the sides of a roast on the stovetop before cooking in a crockpot or oven.

Butterfly: Splitting meat, poultry, or fish in half horizontally without cutting all the way through. When spread open, the flat piece looks like a butterfly.

Caramelize: Melting and cooking sugar over low heat until it browns. "Caramelization" also refers to the browning that occurs during cooking.

Chiffonade: Thinly sliced strips or shreds of vegetables or herbs.

Cream: Rapidly mixing one or more ingredients with a spoon or mixer until smooth and creamy. When you cream butter or other fats, the mixture also becomes fluffy because air is incorporated during the rapid mixing process.

Curdle: Separation of a mixture into a liquid with solid particles. For example, soured milk curdles.

Deglaze: Adding a liquid to a pan in which food has been browned, and heating it to loosen the cooked food particles. This liquid is usually thickened to make a flavourful sauce.

Dice: To dice is like to chop, but the pieces are smaller.

Dredge: Coating a food lightly with flour, breadcrumbs, or cornmeal.

French: Cutting a meat or vegetable lengthwise into very thin strips.

Grate: To reduce to fragments, shreds, or powder by rubbing against an abrasive surface often a kitchen tool called a 'grater.'

Julienne: To cut a fruit or vegetable into matchstick strips about 2 inches long.

Marinate: To take food and soak it in a mixture of spices, oil, and possibly vinegar to make it more tender and flavourful. You can generally marinate food for half an hour to days depending on the dish.

Mince: Cutting food into very fine pieces.

Reduce: Boiling a liquid in an uncovered pot or pan to evaporate some of the liquid. This reduces the volume, concentrates the flavour, and thickens the mixture.

Sauté: Cooking and stirring a food in a small amount of fat over direct heat.

Score: To make shallow cuts in the surface of a food just before cooking or baking.

Sear: Using high heat to quickly brown the surface of a food to seal in the juices. Foods can be seared in a very hot pan or under the broiler.

Slicing: Is when you cut completely through an object. Think of slicing cheese, or bread. Same principle goes for vegies, meat and fruit.

Simmer: Slowly cooking food in a liquid just below the boiling point. Tiny bubbles may break the surface.

Steam: Steaming is the cooking of foods by steam (moist heat) under varying degrees of pressure.

Steep: Soaking dry ingredients in a hot liquid to infuse it with flavour and colour, as with tea or coffee.

Sweat: Cooking food over low heat in a small amount of fat in a covered pot or pan so it cooks in its own juices until soft but not browned.

Zest: The peel or coloured part of citrus fruit skin, which contains flavourful oils. (The white pith is not part of the zest, and has a bitter taste.)

Kitchen Safety & Hygiene Tips for Kids

Cooking is a life skill and provides kids with a hands-on experience that teaches a valuable lifelong skill. Engaging kids in the kitchen at an early age builds a strong foundation for successful cooking practices. Safety is a big part of cooking. Set the ground rules before your child picks up his first whisk or spatula. The kitchen is full of potential dangers, making it essential to teach your child how to behave in the area.

Clean Hands

The first line of defence against germs is to WASH YOUR HANDS! Good hand washing is the first line of defence against the spread of many illnesses, from the common cold to more serious illnesses such as meningitis, bronchiolitis, influenza, hepatitis A, and most types of infectious diarrhea.

Supervision

With knives, appliances and heat sources in the kitchen, adult supervision is a must for any cooking activity with kids. An adult can help assess the potential dangers and keep the kids from them. An adult in the kitchen also ensures the kids will use the kitchen equipment properly and practice the other kitchen safety rules.

Restricted Activities

The ages of the kids involved influences what kitchen activities they can handle. Assess your child's age and maturity level to determine which kitchen duties should be restricted for them. Younger kids shouldn't handle sharp knives because of the potential of cuts, but they might be able to handle a dull butter knife if it will do. If a sharp knife is necessary, an adult should handle the cutting. The use of the stove and oven should be reserved for older kids.

Proper Utensil Usage

Kids need to practice using all kitchen utensils and appliances properly. Demonstrate how to use utensils, such as spatulas, whisks and egg beaters. Think about the types of utensils you use on a regular basis in the kitchen and include them in the demonstration. Do the same with small appliances, such as mixers, blenders and toasters. Using these tools might seem like common knowledge, but kids might not know all of the proper uses and safety rules for them.

Food Handling

Kids also need guidance on proper food handling. If they are helping with meals that involve meat, instruct them on the importance of washing your hands and the work area after preparing the meat. Emphasise that no other foods should go on the surfaces until they are clean. Storing cold foods in the refrigerator is another important lesson for the kids. Teach them to put leftovers in the refrigerator right away so harmful bacteria doesn't form.

Cleaning

Cleaning the kitchen properly is a matter of safety that kids should address. Leaving remnants of food can lead to contamination of other food items. Show kids how to clean the surfaces and remind them to clean immediately after finishing the task. Discuss where different waste materials go. If you have a compost bin, teach them which items go in it. If you recycle, talk to the kids about the packaging and items that can be reused or recycled.

Plastic Utensils

Plastic spatulas, measuring cups, bowls and dishes will come in handy and you'll have help in the kitchen.

Kitchen Best-Practices

- *Always turn handles inward when cooking on the stovetop — away from prying fingers*
- *Never place hot food or drinks on a surface that kids can reach*
- *Always have an adult present for the 'unexpecteds!'*
- *Keep it simple and have fun!*

Healthy Habits

To help you choose foods with the right mix of essential nutrients for your growing kids, the Australian Healthy Eating Guidelines recommend basing your diet on the Five Food Groups. To stay healthy, it's recommended you eat a certain number of serves from each of these five groups every day.

FOOD GROUP	DAILY SERVES
Vegetables	5
Breads, cereals, rice, pasta and noodles	5–9
Fruit	2
Milk, yoghurt and cheese	2–4
Meat, fish, poultry, eggs, nuts and legumes	1–2

An Active Life

Childhood obesity is one of the most serious public health challenges of the 21st century. You've probably all heard the statistics from around the world; a quick 'Google' search tells you that 1 in 4 children in Australia are overweight, 1 in 3 in the USA and rates growing at an alarming pace.

While many factors contribute to this, here are some practical suggestions we have learnt to help fight obesity from a variety of both health experts and active families.

1. **Play:** Encourage your kids and grandkids to get at least 60 minutes of daily physical activity every single day.

2. **Let your children have their say:** Get them involved in your weekly menus, the more input and interest they display, the more likelihood you have of getting them to eat their meals (or *hopefully* at least to try them).

3. **Unplug at meal times:** We know it's so very hard to turn off the TV, and leave the iPhone or iPad in the office for meals … But we have to TRY! Try to have at least one sit-down meal every day together as a family, use this as your time for conversation and connection.

4. **Keep it on hand:** Keep a supply of nutritious snack foods like fruit, vegies, nuts, legumes, whole-grain crackers, breads and cereals on hand. Cut them into bite-sized pieces to make them more inviting, a child is more likely to grab a piece of watermelon than a watermelon.

5. **Be a good role model:** 'Monkey see; Monkey do.' Set a good example by serving reasonable portions, eating lots of fresh fruits and vegies, drinking lots of water and exercising daily (mental note; must walk more regularly!)

6. **Eat Breakfast:** Of all the meals do not skip brekky as it is the most important meal of the day. Not only is brekky linked to better brain function in kids, it also jump starts the metabolism.

7. **Cut down on:** TV, computer and video games and sitting for more than 30 minutes at a time.

8. **3-5 times a week try and fit in some 'aerobic' activity:** Jogging, rollerblading, skateboarding, volleyball, netball, soccer, rugby or whatever ativity that gets your heart rate 'up.'

9. **2-3 times a week engage in 'leisure' activities:** Tennis, canoeing, bike riding, fishing, surfing, swimming or whatever activity gets you up and active.

10. **EVERYDAY:** Play outside, take the stairs rather than the elevator, do some gardening for Mum, pick up the vaccum cleaner, help out around the house, walk the dog and SMILE!

Top 4 Rules to encourage Healthier Eating Habits

- *The better the parents eat, the better their kids will eat*
- *Let fruit and vegetables reign in your kitchen and on your plates*
- *Focus on the quality not the quantity, trust your kid's appetite*
- *Do not give up; often several exposures may be required to get your kids to try a new food … Keep it fun and relaxed!*

4 The Baby

A baby will make love stronger
Days shorter, nights longer
Bank roll smaller
Home happier, clothes shabbier
The past forgotten
And the future worth living for.

Anonymous

Baked Apples

SERVES 1

- *1 sweet delicious apple, cored*
- *½ tsp. butter*
- *1/8 tsp. cinnamon*

Preheat oven 180°C. Place the butter in the core and sprinkle with cinnamon. Place in a shallow baking dish with ½ cup (125ml) of water. Bake for 30 minutes or until tender (top–up with water if needed). Allow to cool before removing the skin and mashing.

Blueberry, Peach & Pear Rice

SERVES 3

- *1 ripe, juicy peach, skinned, stoned and chopped*
- *1 medium, ripe pear, peeled, cored and chopped*
- *¼ cup (50g) blueberries*
- *2–3 tbs. baby rice cereal*

Put the fruit into a small saucepan, cover with a lid and cook over a low heat for 3–4 minutes, stirring occasionally. Puree in a blender and stir in the baby rice while still hot.

Dreamy Creamy Carrots

SERVES 2

Recipe from Hayley at the Bub Hub.

- *½ medium carrot*
- *1 tbs. baby rice cereal*
- *8 tbs. breastmilk or formula*

Peel and dice carrot finely. Cover in a little water and simmer until very tender, drain and puree. Blend the carrot with baby rice and milk. Serve warm.

Hint: Single serves of carrot puree can be frozen in an ice cube tray and sealed in a plastic bag.

Parsnip & Pear Puree

SERVES 2

- *1 parsnip, peeled and diced*
- *1 ripe pear, skin, seeds and core removed*

Steam parsnip until tender, then add pear for final 2 minutes of steaming. Mash ingredients and serve.

"May you live as long as you want and Never want as long as you live."

Irish Blessing

Peach & Banana Puree

SERVES 1

- *1 ripe peach, skinned, stoned and cut into pieces*
- *1 small banana, peeled and sliced*
- *½ tbs. apple juice*
- *1 tsp. baby rice cereal*

Put the peach and banana into a small pan together with the apple juice, cover with a lid and simmer for 2–3 minutes, then puree. If the puree is too runny, stir in a little baby rice.

Pear & Apple with Cinnamon

SERVES 4

- *2 apples, peeled and chopped*
- *2 ripe pears, peeled and chopped*
- *4 tbs. (60ml) apple juice or water*
- *A generous pinch of ground cinnamon*

Put the fruit into a saucepan together with the apple juice or water and cinnamon (if using), cover with a lid and cook over a low heat for 6–8 minutes or until tender. Blend the fruit into a smooth puree.

Prune & Apple Puree

SERVES 4

Recipe from Hayley at the Bub Hub.

- *3 large apples, cored, peeled and cut into quarters*
- *½ cup (80g) prunes, pitted*
- *¼ cup (60ml) apple juice*

Put all ingredients in a large saucepan and simmer over medium heat for 20–30 minutes or until apples are tender. Puree with food processor.

Tip: Prunes are sweet and rich in fibre. Babies LOVE them and they are brilliant for relieving constipation.

Strawberry, Peach & Pear Crumble

SERVES 2

- *½ cup (75g) strawberries, hulled and quartered*
- *1 large, juicy ripe peach, skinned, stoned and cut into pieces*
- *1 large ripe pear, peeled, cored and cut into pieces*
- *1 baby organic rusk*

Put the fruit into a small, heavy-based saucepan, cover with a lid and simmer for about 3 minutes. Crush the rusk (place in a plastic bag and crush with a rolling pin), then blend the fruit together with the crushed rusk.

Sweet Potato & Broccoli

SERVES 3

- *200g sweet potato, peeled and diced*
- *75g broccoli, cut into florets*
- *1–2 tbs. breastmilk or formula*

Steam the sweet potato and broccoli until tender (the sweet potato for about 12 minutes; broccoli for 7–8 minutes). Alternatively, place the sweet potato in a saucepan, cover with water and boil for 4 minutes, then add the broccoli and continue to boil for 7–8 minutes. Puree together with the milk.

Root Vegie Puree

SERVES 6

- *200g sweet potato, peeled and chopped*
- *200g carrots, peeled and chopped*
- *110g parsnips, peeled and chopped*

Steam the vegetables for about 20 minutes or until tender. Blend to a puree, adding a little of the boiled water from the bottom of the steamer to bring it to the right consistency.

The Cooking Poem

When you're cooking in the kitchen,
You're learning all the while
To pour and measure, mix and stir
And sift flour into a pile.

Scrub your hands before you start
Then gather up the gear
Like pots'n pans and measuring cups
That you use throughout the year.

Go over the recipe, step-by-step,
So you'll know just what to do.
By carefully following the directions,
It won't be hard for you.

Have a hot pad handy
And an adult standing by
So you won't hurt yourself
When using the stove or baking a pie.

Besides the fun and learning,
There's always cleaning up to do,
And even though it's quite a chore,
It's part of cooking too.

But after all the work is done,
It will soon be time for dinner.
And when someone asks for seconds,
You'll know you've cooked a winner!

www.childstoryhour.com

What's 4 Brekky?

Research has clearly shown that children who consistently eat breakfast test higher in most academic areas.

EAT YOUR BREAKFAST!

Bacon, Egg & Cheese Croissants

SERVES 4

f **Maureen Lintvelt: facebook.com/4ingredientspage**

- *4 croissants*
- *1 cup bacon or ham, cut into small pieces*
- *1 cup (100g) cheese, grated*
- *1 large egg, seasoned*

Preheat oven to 200°C. Mix last 3 ingredients in bowl. Slice croissants, open horizontally and spoon in the mixture. Bake for approximately 12–15 minutes. Serve immediately.

Tip: 12 mini-croissants will work too.

JOKE

Why did the man at the orange juice factory lose his job?

Because he couldn't concentrate!

Baked Apples with Raspberry Crunch

SERVES 4

Recipe by Melinda Salmond.

- *2 large apples, peeled, remove seeds and cut into wedges*
- *1 cup frozen raspberries*
- *¾ cup mixed fruit muesli (crush if needed for younger toddlers)*
- *¼ cup (80g) maple syrup*

Preheat oven to 180°C. Line a baking tray with baking paper. Lay apple wedges on baking tray and top with berries. Sprinkle muesli over, then drizzle with maple syrup. Bake for 15 minutes, or until tops are golden and fruit is tender.

Optional: Absolutely amazing with ice-cream (well maybe not for breakfast!)

Banana Fritters

SERVES 4

Our children loooove these.

- *1 cup (175g) self raising flour*
- *1 egg*
- *1 cup (250ml) milk*
- *4 small bananas (or 2 large, cut in half)*

Mix flour and egg with a pinch of salt. Beat, gradually adding milk until thick and smooth. Dunk the bananas into the batter and then fry in a non-stick frying pan until the batter turns a light golden brown all over.

Optional: Don't be stingy if you are serving these with a drizzle of pure maple syrup. The Maple Tree is antioxidant rich, that is why the syrup is full of minerals like zinc, calcium and thiamine ... Now that's sweet!

Banana-Bix Shake

MAKES 4

www **Recipe from Maria Mikhail.**

- *1 banana*
- *1 ½ cups (375ml) milk*
- *1 weet bix*
- *1 tsp. honey*

Pop all ingredients into a blender and blend until smooth …
As Maria says "Hey Presto! The kids will love it!"

Berry Blast Brekky

SERVES 1

Recipe by Chellie Mantell.

- *¼ cup raw berry muesli*
- *¼ cup (60ml) cloudy apple juice*
- *½ green or pink lady apple, grated*
- *1 tbs. natural yoghurt*

Soak the muesli and apple juice overnight in a small bowl. In the
morning when ready to serve, stir in the grated apple and top
with yoghurt!

Breakfast Soup

SERVES 2

- *¾ cup (200g) vanilla yoghurt*
- *½ cup banana, cubed*
- *½ cup peaches, peeled and chopped*
- *¼ cup wheat germ*

Blend together and top with additional wheat germ.

Optional: For toddlers over 12 months, add 1 teaspoon of honey.

'Energy-Boosting' Breakfast

SERVES 2

- *2 pieces raisin toast*
- *½ tsp. butter*
- *1 banana, mashed*
- *1 tbs. honey*

Spread raisin toast with butter and mashed banana, and drizzle with honey to serve.

Tip: Bananas provide energy from carbohydrates as well as being a source of fibre and many vitamins and minerals.

"You need to eat food to keep your brain running"

Riley, aged 5

Flat Hash Brown

MAKES 12

- *4 potatoes (800g), peeled*
- *1¼ cups (125g) cheddar cheese, grated*
- *2 tbs. (30ml) vegetable oil*

Coarsely grate potatoes, use your hands to squeeze out as much excess liquid as possible. Add the grated cheese. Place a quarter cup measurement of the mixture on a baking paper-lined baking tray. Heat two tsp. of oil in a large non-stick frying pan. Place two portions of the potato mixture in the pan and flatten each with a spatula. Cook over a medium heat until browned. Turn and cook the other side. Repeat with remaining mixture.

Hint: Serve as part of a breakfast or brunch or served topped with smoked salmon, dill and cream cheese ... Yummy!

Fruit Cocktail Muffins

MAKES 12

These are ideal for breakfast when in a hurry ... Grab and Go!

- *2 cups (350g) self raising flour*
- *1 cup (200g) caster sugar*
- *410g can fruit cocktail, undrained*

Preheat oven to 150°C. Line the muffin tray with muffin papers. In a large bowl, add flour and sugar and stir well. Add the undrained fruit cocktail and stir until just combined. Spoon into muffin papers and bake for 20 minutes or until the muffin tops are golden brown and a wooden skewer inserted into the centre comes out clean.

Tip: Store any leftover muffins in an airtight container for up to 3 days.

Ham & Cheese Breakfast Wraps

SERVES 1

- *1 egg*
- *2 slices of honey ham, thinly sliced*
- *1 tbs. cheese, grated*
- *1 soft tortilla*

Whisk egg and 3 tbs. water in a small bowl. Heat a small non-stick pan and scramble the egg and ham for 2 minutes, or until cooked through. Warm the tortilla in the microwave for 10 seconds and spoon the mixture onto the tortilla. Sprinkle with cheese and wrap by folding the bottom up first to stop any spilling, then fold either side over the top. Serve as is or toasted for a delicious and nutritious breakfast.

Optional: Add in any of your child's favourite chopped vegies!

Healthy Omelette

MAKES 2

- *3 eggs, beaten*
- *½ cup (50g) cheese, grated*
- *1 tsp. parsley, finely chopped*
- *1 tbs. (15g) butter*

Into eggs, lightly fold in 3 tbs. cold water, then cheese and parsley. Melt butter in a non-stick pan and when hot pour in the mixture. Cook until golden brown underneath. Brown top under griller, or turn with an egg flipper and cook until lightly golden all over.

Tip: Plant a herb in a small pot with your child. Parsley is the world's most popular herb and is very useful to have on hand. Mint is also a great herb to plant, as it is very hard to kill!

Homemade Peanut Butter

MAKES 1 CUP

- *1½ cups unsalted, roasted peanuts, skins on*
- *1–2 tbs. peanut oil*

Mix the peanuts with the peanut oil, and pour the mixture into the food processor, add a sprinkling of salt. Process the mixture until it's very smooth. Store in a sealed container in the fridge, best eaten within 2 weeks.

Optional: For Chunky Peanut Butter, remove ¼ cup from your peanuts and set them aside. Mix the rest of the peanuts with the oil, and pour the mixture into the food processor. Process the mixture until it's very smooth, then stir in the peanuts that you had set aside. Process a few seconds more to create the chunks in your chunky peanut butter.

Nutella Crêpes

MAKES 6

These really are Gooood!

- *1 egg, beaten*
- *1 cup (250ml) milk*
- *1 cup (175g) plain flour*
- *6 tbs. nutella*

Mix together egg, milk, 1 cup (250ml) water and the flour until smooth. Pour a-quarter cup of mixture into a non-stick pan and swirl in a circular motion outwards so the batter is even. Cook for about 2 minutes or until the bottom is light brown. Flip and cook the other side, remove and spread with 1 tbs. nutella, roll and cut in half to serve. Repeat until all the mixture is gone.

You Tube *4 Ingredients Channel/Nutella Crêpes*

Peanut Butter & Banana Wraps

MAKES 2

A recipe from Wendy Beattie.

- *2 whole-meal wraps*
- *2 tbs. peanut butter*
- *2 tsp. honey*
- *1 ripe banana, mashed*

Spread peanut butter and honey onto the wrap. Spread with banana, fold up bottom third and roll. Toast in a sandwich press for 1–2 minutes.

Raspberry Jam Omelette

MAKES 4

For a morning boost infuse your breakfast with a soft citrus flavours.

- *1 tbs. (15ml) olive oil*
- *4 large eggs*
- *¼ cup (60ml) fresh orange juice*
- *⅓ cup (110g) raspberry jam*

Mist the bottom and sides of a medium non-stick frying pan with the oil and heat on medium. Meanwhile whisk together eggs, juice and a pinch of salt. Pour egg mixture into hot pan. Cook, occasionally lifting the edge until golden on base and no longer runny on the surface, for approximately 5 minutes. Spread jam across the surface and gently fold omelette in half. Cook for 2 minutes then slide onto a plate, cut into wedges and serve.

Optional: Serve with a dollop of yoghurt and sprinkle of cinnamon.

You Tube *4 Ingredients Channel/Raspberry Jam Omlette*

Sausage & Egg Muffin

MAKES 2

- *2 sausages*
- *2 eggs*
- *2 English muffins*
- *2 slices of cheddar cheese*

Squeeze the inside of the sausages into a bowl and form into
2 patties. In a medium, non-stick frying pan, fry for 4 minutes
each side or until done. Set aside. In the same pan, fry the eggs.
Split the muffin and toast both slices. Top one half of the muffin
with a pattie, a slice of cheese and an egg. Place other half of
muffin on top, press gently and **enjoy!**

Sunny Scrambled Eggs

SERVES 2

- *2 eggs*
- *1 tbs. (15g) butter*
- *2 tbs. (30ml) milk*
- *2 pieces of toast buttered, and cut into soldiers*

Crack the eggs into a large bowl, season with salt and pepper
and whisk. Melt the butter over medium heat in a saucepan.
Pour in the eggs and milk and stir constantly until the mixture
starts to set but is still wobbly. Spoon a mound into the centre
of a plate and arrange toast around the egg to look like a ray
of sunshine!

Vegemite & Avocado Soldiers

SERVES 1

- *1 slice whole-grain bread*
- *½ tsp. butter*
- *½ tsp. vegemite*
- *¼ ripe avocado, mashed*

Toast the bread and lightly spread with butter, then vegemite and avocado. Cut into 3 soldiers, or little squares if it's easier for your baby or toddler to eat!

Hint: Eating breakfast regularly also establishes a normal eating pattern which is the key to maintaining a healthy weight.

Volcanic Eggs

MAKES 4

Recipe from Cheryl Jensen.

- *4 eggs, separated*
- *4 slices hi-fibre bread, remove crusts*
- *1 cup (100g) parmesan cheese, grated*

Using an electric beater, beat egg whites until stiff peaks form (similar to a meringue). Lay each slice of bread onto a paper-lined baking tray and onto each spoon a mound of egg white, then make a little crevice on the very top for the egg yolk. Sprinkle with parmesan and a grind of black pepper (which is the volcanic ash ☺). Bake in a 180°C oven for 8–12 minutes or until just brown.

Tip: Cheryl wrote; "The egg white should be firm, the cheese melted and the egg yolk runny when you cut into it. Takes a little while, but it's worth it!"

The Challenge

Have your kids write down the date and
what their most favourite breakfasts are.

_____

Snack Attack

Knock Knock.
Who's there?
Ice cream!
Ice cream who?
Ice cream if you don't let me in ☺.

Ants on Logs

MAKES 12

A golden oldie!

- *2 celery stalks, top 'n' tailed and destringed*
- *6 tsp. cream cheese*
- *⅔ cup (50g) sultanas*

Cut celery into bite-sized pieces. Fill the hollow with cream cheese and sprinkle with sultanas or 'ants.'

Apple & Peanut Butter Pizzas

MAKES 12

- *2 Granny Smith apples, cored*
- *1 cup (230g) peanut butter*
- *¼ cup (30g) flaked coconut*
- *¼ cup (30g) toasted muesli (or granola)*

Cut each apple crosswise into 6 rounds. Spread with peanut butter. Sprinkle half with coconut and half with muesli.

Optional: Other nice toppings would be sultanas and dried cranberries.

Apricot Baskets

SERVES 4

- 4 ripe apricots
- ¼ cup (65g) cottage cheese
- 1 tsp. cinnamon
- 2 tbs. honey

Halve and stone each apricot and fill with cottage cheese. Add a sprinkle of cinnamon and drizzle with honey.

Tip: Apricots range from pale yellow to golden orange and some have a soft red blush. They have a soft, velvety skin and a sweet, juicy taste. They are delicious eaten raw or baked, poached, grilled or stewed.

Blueberry Dipper

SERVES 1

- ¾ cup (185g) vanilla yoghurt
- ½ cup (75g) blueberries, pureed
- 4 tbs. honey
- ½ pineapple, cut into long narrow wedges

Combine the first three ingredients and serve with the pineapple wedges to dip.

Tip: This is a great way to get kids to eat blueberries or 'brain-berries' as they are fondly known.

Caramel Popcorn

SERVES 6

Popcorn = easy and economical

- *8 cups popped popcorn*
- *½ cup (160g) honey*
- *½ cup (130g) smooth peanut butter*
- *3 tbs. (45g) butter*

Boil honey in a small saucepan for 5 minutes. Stir in peanut butter and butter. Pour over popped corn and stir.

Optional: Add 1 tsp. vanilla to the mix in the saucepan.

Chewy Flapjacks

MAKES 12

An easy variation to an Anzac biscuit!

- *¾ cup (175g) butter*
- *¼ cup (50g) caster sugar*
- *⅓ cup (120g) golden syrup*
- *2¾ cups (250g) rolled oats*

Preheat oven to 180°C. Line the base and sides of a 20cm square cake tin with baking paper. Mix butter, sugar and syrup in a pan and heat gently until the butter has melted. Add the oats and stir until all the ingredients are combined. Turn the mixture into the tin and level the surface. Bake for 15–20 minutes or until just golden. Leave to cool slightly before cutting into fingers and storing in an airtight container.

Tip: Kids need at least one hour a day of activity. For kids who aren't as active as you would like, try promoting 'activity' rather than exercise … Sometimes it's all about the 'words' we use.

Chipwiches

MAKES 8

On a recent trip to New York we learnt about the simple pleasures of a 'Chipwich'.

- *16 round chocolate chip biscuits*
- *250g tub of your favourite ice-cream*

Onto a serving plate, lay 8 chocolate chip cookies, flat side up. Onto each cookie, place a nice spherical scoop of ice-cream. Top with remaining cookies and serve immediately.

Optional: If in cooler climes, substitute cold ice-cream for your kid's favourite icing or frosting.

Choc-Coated Ritz

MAKES 24

Thanks to 'Rose' who shared this with Kim on a P&O Lifestyle Cruise, February 2011.

- *150g milk chocolate*
- *24 Ritz crackers*

In a microwave-proof container melt your chocolate on high, checking and stirring every 20 seconds until it is nice and runny. Line a baking tray with baking paper. Dunk the crackers, one-by-one to ¾ coat. Hold for 10 seconds to allow excess chocolate to drip away. Lay coated crackers on prepared tray and chill before serving to the squeals of delight from kids (*big and small!*)

Cinnamon Chips

SERVES 6

- *10 flour tortillas*
- *½ cup (115g) butter, melted*
- *½ cup cinnamon sugar*

Preheat oven to 160°C. Brush both sides of each tortilla generously with butter, then sprinkle the top side with cinnamon sugar. Cut into wedges and arrange in a single layer on a large baking sheet. Bake for 8–10 minutes.

Optional: These are delicious served with Fruit Salsa (p.38) or yummy dips.

Date Balls

MAKES 24

Recipe from Glenyis Cordie.

- *200g dates, pitted*
- *⅔ cup (80g) walnuts or almonds*
- *40g mixed seeds (sunflower, pepitas, sesame)*
- *½ cup (60g) coconut (plus extra for rolling)*

Place dates, nuts, seeds and coconut into a food processor. Process for about 1 minute, until well chopped but not pulverised. Scoop out 1 teaspoon at a time and form into balls and roll in coconut. Refrigerate for at least 30 minutes until firm.

Optional: Roll in sesame seeds instead.

Edible Vegie Bowl

SERVES 6

- *1 red capsicum, washed*
- *2 stalks celery, washed and strings removed*
- *1 carrot, washed and peeled*

Your kid's favourite dip (see: Lunchbox Fun-du p. 56) Cut the capsicum in half (from tip to toe). Remove seeds and membrane from both sides. Keeping one half as your 'edible bowl' cut the other half into dipping sticks. Slice the carrot and celery the same. Pop some dip into the bottom of the capsicum bowl, then put celery, carrot and capsicum slices into the bowl for a portable vegie treat!

Tip: Keep nutrition fun so kids will enjoy being healthy, try to be creative. A slice of pineapple, for example, may be met with more enthusiasm when called a 'pineapple chip.'

Fruit Salsa

MAKES 8

- *1 cup diced strawberries*
- *1 banana, diced*
- *1 kiwi fruit, sliced and diced*
- *1 mandarin, peeled and segmented*

Combine fruits in a medium serving bowl and toss gently.

Optional: Serve drizzled with 2 tbs. lemon juice, and a sprinkling of cinnamon and nutmeg.

Green Pita Dippers

SERVES 6

- 3 tbs. (45g) butter, softened
- 1 tbs. Gourmet Garden Coriander
- 1 tsp. Gourmet Garden Garlic
- 4 whole-wheat pitas

Preheat oven to 180°C. Line a baking tray with baking paper. Place the first 3 ingredients in a bowl and season with salt. Mix until combined, then spread over each pita bread. Cut into wedges and place on baking tray. Bake for 8 minutes or until golden.

Jatz Sandwiches

MAKES 8

- 16 Jatz biscuits
- 2 slices cheddar cheese, quartered
- 8 thin slices kabana
- 8 thin slices cucumber

Place 8 Jatz biscuits onto a serving plate. Top with a square of cheese, a round of cucumber and a slice of kabana. Top each with remaining Jatz and serve.

Optional: Jatz are easily interchangeable with Ritz crackers.

Microwave Fudge

MAKES 12

This is *simply sensational* and you don't even have to turn on the oven!

- *2 cups chocolate chips*
- *400g can condensed milk*
- *1½ cups (180g) walnuts, chopped*

In a microwave-proof bowl, melt chocolate on medium/high stirring every 30 seconds or until nice and smooth. Gradually add condensed milk, stirring vigorously all the while. Add nuts and stir to combine. Spread in a paper-lined 18cm square cake tin. Refrigerate for 1 hour or until set. Cut into squares to serve.

Tip: All nuts are an important component of the healthy eating pyramid. The special thing about walnuts, is that they not only look like our wrinkled brains but they are very good for our wrinkled brains, as they are high in omega-3 fat.

Taco Popcorn

SERVES 6–8

- *8 cups popped popcorn*
- *3 tbs. (45g) butter, melted*
- *2 tsp. taco seasoning mix (or to taste)*

Pop popcorn into a large bowl. Mix together butter and taco seasoning (start with 1 tsp. and taste before adding more). Drizzle over popcorn. Toss to coat thoroughly. Serve immediately.

Tapas for Kids

SERVES 4

- *100g honey smoked ham, cut into strips*
- *12 cheddar cheese cubes*
- *½ fresh rockmelon, cut into chunks*
- *A bunch of seedless red grapes*

Arrange all on a serving plate and place it prominently where kids gather or pass to graze on.

Tip: Tapas are a fun way to offer a variety of healthy snacks to kids; adding fresh seasonal fruit cut into bite-sized pieces is not only colourful but inviting too.

Zesty Shortbread Stars

MAKES 40

- *2 cups (350g) plain flour, sifted*
- *1 cup (200g) icing sugar, firmly packed*
- *Zest of 1 orange*
- *250g butter, softened*

Mix flour, icing sugar and orange peel. Add butter and mix until crumbly. Work the dough with your hands until it holds together. Refrigerate for 30 minutes. Roll dough out onto a clean, floured surface until about 1cm thick. Use a variety of star-shaped pastry cutters to cut 40 stars from the dough. Place on paper-lined trays and place in the freezer for 15 minutes to chill. Bake for 12–15 minutes or until golden. Cool before serving.

Optional: Drizzle shortbread with melted chocolate to serve.

The Challenge

Have your kids draw their favouite Snack Attack ideas!

What's 4 Lunch?

*The children were lined up in the cafeteria
of a Catholic elementary school for lunch.
At the head of the table was a large pile of apples.
The nun made a note, and posted on the apple tray:
"Take only ONE. God is watching."
Moving further along the lunch line, at the other end
of the table was a large pile of chocolate chip cookies.
A child had written a note,
"Take all you want. God is watching the apples."*

Apple & Sultana Wrap

MAKES 1

- *1–2 tbs. cinnamon or vanilla yoghurt*
- *1 whole-grain tortilla*
- *¼ cup stewed apples*
- *2 tsp. sultanas*

Spread yoghurt down the centre of the wrap, leaving room on the sides and a little on the top and bottom. Top with apple and sprinkle with sultanas. Fold the top and bottom in, and roll from the sides to completely enclose the filling. Cut in half to serve!

Optional: Substitute cream cheese for yoghurt and toast in a sandwich press until lightly golden. You can also use fruit like blueberries, pear or mashed banana as a lovely substitute for apples.

Tip: If you have leftover stewed or canned apples, use as a topper on breakfast cereals, or in the extremely popular Apple Slice recipe from 4 Ingredients 2.

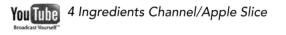 *4 Ingredients Channel/Apple Slice*

Bagel Bites

MAKES 16

Bagels can be served in many ways, here is one of our favourites.

- *2 bagels (use old ones if you have them)*
- *2 rindless bacon rashers, diced*
- *4 tbs. pizza sauce*
- *1 cup (100g) mozzarella cheese, shredded*

Preheat oven to 180°C. Into a small frying pan, place bacon and cook for 4–5 minutes or until just crisping. Meanwhile, split bagels in half horizontally and with a spoon, hollow out some of the bread. Divide the pizza sauce among each, then the bacon and then the cheese. Bake for 10–12 minutes or until the cheese is golden and melted. Remove from oven, cool slightly before slicing into quarters to serve.

Optional: Change your fillings to whatever your kids will eat. Try BBQ sauce, top with shredded chicken, chopped capsicum, onion and cheese. Try tomato sauce and mustard, kabana and cheese.

Bacon & Banana Fingers

MAKES 4

- *3 rashers rindless bacon, diced*
- *4 thick slices bead*
- *1 large banana*
- *½ cup (50g) cheddar cheese, grated*

Crisp fry bacon. Toast bread under the grill on one side only. Remove and place on a paper-lined baking tray, untoasted side up. Onto each, slice the banana, sprinkle with bacon and then with cheese. Place under a hot grill for 4–5 minutes or until the cheese has melted and is bubbly. Remove and cut into 'fingers' to serve.

Bread Baskets with Avocado, Bacon & Egg

MAKES 4

This is just so scrummy!

- *4 slices whole-meal bread, crusts removed*
- *4 slices rindless bacon, chopped*
- *1 ripe avocado, halved, then cut into chunks*
- *1 hard-boiled egg, peeled and quartered*

Preheat oven to 200°C. Use a rolling pin to flatten bread. Mould each slice into a non-stick muffin tray. Bake for 6–8 minutes or until crispy. Meanwhile, heat a non-stick frying pan over a medium/high heat and cook the bacon until nice and crispy. When the bread baskets are ready, remove and place on a serving plate. Then add avocado and bacon alternately and top with an egg quarter.

JOKE

What did the strawberry say to the second strawberry?

"How did you get into this jam?"

Cinderella's Pumpkin Soup

SERVES 4

- *1 tbs. (15g) butter*
- *50g leek (white part only), washed and sliced*
- *225g pumpkin or butternut squash, peeled and cut into cubes*
- *2 cups (500ml) vegetable or chicken stock*

Melt the butter in a saucepan and sauté the leek until soft and lightly golden. Add the pumpkin or butternut squash and continue to cook for 2 minutes. Pour over the stock, bring to the boil and then simmer, covered with lid for 30 minutes or until the pumpkin is tender. Puree in a blender, or mash with a fork for older babies and children.

Tip: Suitable for freezing.

Chicken & Mozzarella Melts

SERVES 4

- *½ BBQ chicken, shredded*
- *4 slices ciabatta*
- *1 avocado, peeled and sliced*
- *1 cup (100g) mozzarella cheese, grated*

Preheat the grill to high. Grill one side of the ciabatta slices until just golden. Remove and on uncooked sides, spread the chicken evenly and top with avocado and mozzarella cheese. Place under grill for 3 minutes or until the cheese is golden and bubbling.

Chunky Corn Chowder

SERVES 4–6

- *1 pkt spring vegetable soup mix*
- *220g can corn kernels*
- *350g potatoes, peeled and diced*
- *¾ cup (185ml) milk*

Combine 1 litre of water and soup mix in a saucepan and stir well. Heat and bring to the boil. Add potatoes and corn, and reduce heat to simmer for 15 minutes or until the potatoes are soft. Add the milk and cook for another 5 minutes. Scoop out some of the vegies and set aside. Blend the rest of the soup in a blender or food processor until smooth. Return to saucepan and add vegies, stir, season and serve.

Optional: Try adding some smoked fish at the time the milk is added for a tasty twist.

'Easy Make-Ahead' Quiche

SERVES 4

- *6 eggs, beaten*
- *4 slices of ham*
- *¼ cup (25g) Parmesan cheese, grated*
- *2 tomatoes, seeds discarded, finely diced*

Preheat oven to 180°C. Mix all ingredients well. Pour into the cups of a greased non-stick muffin tray and bake for 25 minutes or until set. Enjoy immediately or let cool to room temperature, place in a sealed container and store in the fridge.

Tip: Make these delicious quiches the night before.

Green and Gold Fritters

MAKES 8

- 1 cup (175g) self raising flour
- 1 cup (250ml) milk
- 1 free range egg, beaten
- ½ cup frozen peas and corn

Heat a small non-stick frying pan to medium heat. Lightly whisk flour, milk and egg together until there are no lumps. Stir the peas and corn and a little seasoning through the batter. Using a tablespoon, form flat, golf ball sized circles in the pan. Once they begin to bubble evenly, flip and cook the other side until lightly golden.

Hot-Bean-Dogs

MAKES 4

- 4 frankfurters
- 4 long hotdog rolls
- 220g can baked beans
- ½ cup (50g) cheddar cheese, grated

Cook frankfurters in a saucepan of simmering water for 5–7 minutes. Remove and drain. Split rolls lengthways. Place frankfurters in rolls and top with warmed baked beans and a sprinkling of cheese.

Pups In Blankets

MAKES 2

- *2 tbs. mayonnaise*
- *2 slices of lavash bread*
- *2 hot dogs, cooked*
- *¼ cup (25g) cheese, grated*

Preheat oven to 180°C. Spread a little mayonnaise onto the bread, top with the hot dog and cheese and roll into a tube. Place on a baking paper-lined tray and bake for 10 minutes or until the bread starts to crisp and the cheese melts.

Rainbow Fried Rice

MAKES 4

- *1 tbs. (15ml) macadamia oil*
- *¼ cup mixed Asian vegies, diced*
- *¼ cup (50g) cooked brown rice*
- *1 tsp. soy sauce*

Preheat a non-stick frying pan to medium heat and drizzle with oil. Combine remaining ingredients and stir-fry for 4–6 minutes or until vegies soften and are heated through.

Optional: Add some cooked chicken, finely chopped or a sliced egg omelette.

Sesame Sausages

SERVES 4

- 12 chipolatas
- 2 tbs. honey
- 2 tbs. sesame seeds

Preheat oven to 200°C. Scatter sausages over a baking paper-lined tray. Cook for 15 minutes, drain. Drizzle with honey and cook for another 15 minutes, turning a couple of times until the sausages are sticky and golden all over. Sprinkle with sesame seeds and cook for a final 5 minutes.

You Tube *4IngredientsChannel/Sesame Sausages*

Vegie Muffins

MAKES 12

- 2 cups (350g) self raising flour
- 400g can creamed corn (reserve ¼ cup)
- 1 cup (250ml) buttermilk
- 1 cup (100g) cheddar cheese, grated (reserve ¼ cup)

Preheat oven to 180°C. Place flour in a large bowl and make a well. Add all other ingredients, except reserved corn and cheese, and season. Using a large metal spoon, fold until just combined (don't overmix or the muffins will be tough). Spoon the mixture into the cups of a greased muffin tray. Evenly dollop and sprinkle with remaining creamed corn and cheese. Bake for 20 minutes or until the tops are golden and spring back lightly when touched.

Tip: If there isn't enough batter to fill all muffin cups, half fill the empty cups with water. This will help the muffins bake evenly and protect the pan. Some suggest saving one of the cups to hold water to help keep muffins moist and prevent edges from burning while baking.

Wrapped Eggs

MAKES 2

- 4 eggs
- ½ cup (50g) cheddar cheese, grated
- 2 asparagus stalks, finely sliced
- 2 whole-meal tortillas

In a bowl, whisk the eggs and three-quarters of the cheese. Season lightly with salt and pepper. In a small non-stick frying pan, add the eggs and sprinkle with asparagus. Cook for 5 minutes or until soft and moist. Warm the tortilla in a microwave oven then lay it on a flat surface, top with scrambled egg and remaining cheese. Fold in each end of the tortillas and, working from the edge closest to you, roll up each one. Cut in half, or thirds if more manageable, secure with a toothpick and serve.

Zucchini Fritters

SERVES 2

- 2 eggs
- ¼ red onion, grated
- ½ zucchini, grated
- 2 tbs. carrot, grated

Beat eggs and add remaining ingredients, season to taste. Heat a small non-stick frying pan over medium heat. Spoon 2 x 2 tbs. of mixture into the pan, leaving room for spreading. Cook for 2 minutes each side.

Optional: To introduce your children to a little spice serve these dolloped with 1 tsp. sweet chilli sauce mixed into 3 tsp. sour cream.

Lunchboxes

If you have a gem or a tip or a recipe that you include regularly in your lunchbox, please feel free to share it with us and our foodie family at f *facebook/4ingredientspage.*

A good lunchbox should provide your child with enough energy to sustain them all afternoon. It should provide approximately one-third of their recommended daily energy as well as approximately one-third of their daily protein, carbohydrate, fibre and vitamin and mineral requirements.

FRUIT
✓ 1 serving of fruit.

VEGETABLES
✓ 1 serving of vegetables; e.g. carrots, celery, capsicum and cucumber.

DAIRY
✓ 1 serving from this group; e.g. cheese, yoghurt or milk
✓ Alternatively, another calcium-rich food: calcium-fortified soya, tofu, tinned fish, such as tuna, salmon or sardines, or nuts.

PROTEIN
✓ 1 serving of food from the meat, fish or alternative group of protein-rich foods.

CARBOHYDRATES
✓ 1 more serving from the bread, potato and other cereals group.

DRINK
✓ Drink water, and plenty of it.
✓ **Water** is the most important nutrient in our diets and often the most neglected.

Think Inside the Box

Anger is one letter short of Danger!

Eleanor Roosevelt

Aussie Sandwich

MAKES 1 ROUND

- *2 eggs, hard boiled*
- *1 small stick of celery, finely sliced and diced*
- *1 tbs. whole egg mayonnaise*
- *2 slices of bread*

Mash hard-boiled eggs in a bowl. Add celery and mayonnaise and combine well. Spread on bread to form a sandwich.

Caramel Soccer Balls

MAKES 30

- *200g Jersey Caramels*
- *1½ tbs. (25ml) milk*
- *2½ cups (275g) toasted muesli*

In a saucepan over a very low heat, melt caramels with milk stirring until smooth. Add muesli, mix well then cool enough to handle. Take a heaped teaspoon of mixture and roll into balls, place on a tray in the refrigerator to set.

Tip: Damp hands will make rolling these easier.

Chicken Pita

MAKES 1

- ¾ cup (130g) roasted chicken, shredded
- 1 tbs. mayonnaise
- Sprinkle of celery salt
- 1 whole-meal pita

Mix chicken and mayonnaise (add a little extra if needed) then add celery salt. Stuff into pita bread and serve.

Optional: Add a leaf of crisp iceberg lettuce.

Cinnamon Pinwheels

MAKES 20

- ¼ cup (50g) caster sugar
- 2 tsp. ground cinnamon
- 1 sheet puff pastry
- 1 egg, beaten

Preheat oven to 220°C. Line a baking tray with baking paper. Mix the sugar and cinnamon together. Sprinkle half the cinnamon sugar onto the pastry, pressing gently to secure. Brush with egg wash and sprinkle remaining cinnamon sugar. Roll the pastry into a log, brushing the end with a little more egg to secure the edge in place. Cut the log into thin slices and transfer to the prepared baking tray. Bake for 10 minutes or until golden and puffed. Dust with a little extra sugar.

Easy M&M Bars

MAKES 20

These *will* become part of your recipe repertoire.

- *250g pkt arrowroot biscuits*
- *400g can condensed milk*
- *1 cup M & Ms*

Preheat oven to 160°C. Line a baking tray with baking paper. Blend the biscuits in a blender. Add the remaining ingredients and combine well. Scrape the mixture into a baking pan. Bake for 20 minutes. When cooled, cut into bars.

You**Tube** *4ingredientschannel/Easy M&M Bars*
Broadcast Yourself™

Lay it On

MAKES 2

Transform the humble sandwich into a nutritious meal!

- *½ cup (85g) cooked chicken*
- *4 dried apricots, finely diced*
- *2 tbs. whole egg mayonnaise*
- *2 slices multigrain bread*

Mix together chicken, apricots and mayo. Pile onto the first slice of bread, add a lettuce leaf for colour before topping with second slice of bread and slicing to serve.

Lunchbox Fun-Du

Our kids loooove to 'DIP', Here are some of their favourites served with a variety of fruit and vegie dippers.

Corn Relish Dip

SERVES 4

- ½ cup (150g) corn relish
- 300ml sour cream
- 1½ tbs. fresh chives, chopped

Place corn relish, sour cream and 1 tbs. chives in a bowl. Season with salt and pepper. Stir to combine. Serve sprinkled with remaining chives.

'Devonshire' Dip

MAKES ½ CUP

- 125g sour cream
- 2 tbs. strawberry jam

Mix cream and jam together and serve with fresh fruit to dip.

Tomato-Ranch Dip

MAKES 1 CUP

A dip inspired on our latest trip to the USA.

- 250g tub sour cream
- ¼ cup (65g) tomato sauce
- ⅛ tsp. onion powder
- ⅛ tsp. garlic powder

Mix all together and serve in a lunchbox with fresh vegie sticks.

Lunchbox Sushi

SERVES 2

Presents beautifully and are very popular in our households!

- *4 slices soy and linseed bread*
- *1 tbs. whole egg mayonnaise*
- *½ avocado, mashed*
- *4 slices ham*

Remove crusts and, with a rolling pin, gently roll bread to flatten slightly. Along the middle of each slice spread a little mayonnaise and avocado. Lay ham onto each and roll tightly. Cut in thirds, turn up and place into lunchbox for later.

Optional: Use a variety of breads and fillings.

Marshmallow Dream Bar

MAKES 24

- *¼ cup (55g) butter*
- *2 cups marshmallows*
- *½ tsp. vanilla*
- *2½ cups (500g) rice bubbles*

Melt butter in a medium-size saucepan. Add marshmallows and cook over low heat, stirring constantly, until marshmallows are melted and mixture is very syrupy. Remove from heat. Stir in vanilla. Add cereal and stir until well coated. Press warm mixture firmly into buttered 9cm x 13cm pan. Cut into squares when cool.

Optional: Rather than a slice, to make Marshmallow Drops, spoon individual heaped tablespoons of warm marshmallow mixture onto a baking tray. Refrigerate until firm.

Perfect Hard-Boiled Egg

SERVES 2

* *2 eggs*

Place eggs in a saucepan filled with water, covering eggs by at least 2 cm. Bring to boil, cover. Remove from heat, let stand for 15 minutes then transfer eggs into a bowl of ice water to cool. Gently tap eggs to start peeling.

Pinwheel Sandwiches

MAKES 24

Pinwheels are quite pretty and make a nice party tray too.

* *4 whole-meal tortillas, cut in half*
* *125g cream cheese with onion and chives*
* *8 slices fresh ham*
* *2 lettuce leaves, shredded*

Spread the cream cheese on each tortilla half. Top with ham and lettuce. Tightly roll up from left to right. Trim the ends. Wrap in plastic wrap and keep refrigerated. Cut the rolls into 2cm pieces and lay them flat on a plate so they look like pinwheels.

Optional: Make these easy pinwheels using roast chicken, smoked turkey, roast beef or try different flavours of cream cheese or use goat's cheese. Substitute lettuce with spinach, chopped cucumber, avocado or alfalfa. You can even add mustard, salsa, peach or apple preserves.

Purple Pikelets

MAKES 10

Recipe by Jodie Mannion.

- *1 cup (175g) whole-meal self raising flour*
- *1 cup (250ml) milk*
- *1 egg, beaten*
- *½ cup mixed berries*

Heat a small non-stick frying pan to medium heat. Lightly whisk flour, milk and egg together until all lumps are gone. Gently stir berries through mixture. Use a tablespoon to form flat, golf ball sized circles in the pan. Once they begin to bubble evenly, flip and cook the other side until lightly golden.

Optional: Serve dolloped with your kid's favourite yoghurt. Substitute ½ cup of chocolate chips for mixed berries ... Delightful!

Toffee Muesli Bars

MAKES 16

- *½ cup (115g) butter*
- *½ cup (180g) golden syrup*
- *2½ cups (275g) toasted fruit muesli*
- *12 dried apples, diced*

Line a 18cm x 28cm rectangular baking tray with baking paper. Melt the butter and syrup in a medium saucepan. Add muesli and apple and stir to coat. Scrape into the prepared tray and neaten. Cool in the refrigerator for at least 2 hours. Slice to serve.

Trail Mix Ideas

- **Dry snacks:** Select a cereal low in sugar (under 5g per serving), small pretzels, whole-wheat biscuits, rice cake pieces or animal crackers.

- **Dried fruits:** Cherries, apricots, raisins, mangoes or coconut flakes.

  Tip: big pieces of dried fruit can be cut up easily using kitchen scissors.

- **Nuts and seeds:** Sliced almonds, pecan pieces, cashew pieces, pumpkin seeds, sunflower seeds or peanut pieces.

Combine any or all of these ingredients in an airtight container and toss gently to mix. Stored in an airtight container, this will last for weeks.

Zebra Sandwiches

SERVES 2–4

Recipe from Janelle McCosker.

- *4 slices hi-fibre white bread, crusts removed*
- *1½ tbs. (25g) butter*
- *1 tbs. vegemite*

Spread three slices of bread with butter and then Vegemite. Stack the slices, spread side up. Top with unbuttered slice and press gently. Cut in quarters to serve.

Optional: Adding a slice of cheese is a nice option.

Hint: Healthy options are endless when you start with a good bread and a few fresh fillings.

Build a Healthier Sandwich

Ideas from members of our 'foodie-family'
facebook.com/4ingredientspage

- Whole-wheat wrap, tuna, lemon zest and herbed cream cheese
- Whole-wheat baguette, sliced turkey, swiss cheese and grapes
- Toasted grain bread, crisped prosciutto, lettuce, tomato and avocado
- Multi-grain bread, cheddar cheese, mashed avocado, cherry tomatoes sliced
- Toasted English muffin, feta, honey, toasted walnuts finely chopped and fresh basil
- Toasted multi-grain bread, peanut butter, shredded apple, honey
- Multi-grain bread, hard-boiled egg mashed, mayonnaise and lettuce

4 Top Tips when building a Healthier Sandwich

- ✓ Look for at least 2 grams of fibre per slice, with a whole grain listed as the first ingredient.
- ✓ Add protein through meats, fish and beans
- ✓ For hearty, healthy trimmings, add crushed almonds and walnuts
- ✓ The darker the shade of the produce, the greater the antioxidant power; try and include at least '2 colours' in every sandwich.

The Challenge

Describe or draw for your parents
what you enjoy eating during lunchtime at school.

Vegies

When we posed the question on Facebook:
"What works for you getting your children to eat their vegetables?"
Some really clever ideas came back.

We thought you might enjoy the answers.

Angie Covino

Have a make-your-own-pizza or burrito night and cut up a variety of meats, cheeses and vegies such as capsicums, corn, mushrooms, tomatoes, broccoli, etc. Have your child make his own and encourage him to add the colours of the rainbow (good luck with indigo!!!!)

Becky Butler

Don't buy snack foods. Use fruit, vegie sticks and dips, yoghurt, bread or toast for between meal options.

Belinda Pettitt

Mash vegies together and add avacado — avocado is my little ones favourite.

Carla Dooley

My 3 year old was fussy, I found a 'tasting' plate with a colourful variety in small quantities was helpful as she would generally eat most of it.

Jan Neale

Steam and puree cauliflower and add it to milk, butter and some Parmesan cheese to make 'cheese sauce.'

Joanne Baker Tyler

I always grate vegies into anything I cook, my son is a fussy eater when it comes to green vegies, I was too now I eat everything. We discovered the vegie/fruit V8 juice he likes that when I asked him to try it … My mother always said you will get more things done for you by asking not telling!

Joanne Stephens

I had more hassle getting my partner to eat vegies then our little girl! So for him I would grate vegies and add them to his favourite dishes eg., sausage rolls, meatballs and pasta sauces. Now I am able to put them on his plate without complaints lol who would have thought I had to change his habits so our daughter would have healthy ones???

Julie Marie Kurtev

My daughter Ebony loves vegies as she has had her own vegie garden since she was 18 months, now four and a half. She loves being in the garden and everything about it especially cooking from fruit and vegie within. I think leading a good example is very immmortant, fresh is best from garden and tastes yummy.

Kacie Headley

I think the best way to deal with fussy eaters is to start out giving them what they like, for example if its yoghurt, then maybe the next day they have yoghurt with mashed banana, then after that try yogurt, mashed banana and little bit of toasted muesli on top … Baby steps helps, no point trying to force kids, they only dig their heels in harder ☺

Kate Guiver

Keep a bowl of fresh fruits on the counter. Refrigerate ready-to-eat, chopped fruits and vegetables in small bags for easy snacks on the run.

Meagan Moffat

What kids dont luv 2 minute noodles? Soak in boiling water, then add veg. My kids luv peas, corn and capsicum. Green, yellow and red makes it look nice. My 3year old calls it "pretty noodles."

Megan Bullen

PIZZA! The kids get involved helping me making 'healthy' pizzas all the time, here's how: On pita bread spread some pizza sauce. Then top the pizza with corn kernels, red capsicum, mushroom, grated zucchini, ham, chicken & tomato. Sprinkle with cheese and all-purpose seasoning & 'pizza topper.' Mmmmmmm ... and the kids love it!

Melinda Dines

Try serving raw vegies, they are an excellent source of vitamins.

Michelle Evans

Top cereal with freshly chopped fruits or add frozen fruits to smoothies and ice-creams.

Melissa Byrnes Pearce

I would make a beef macaroni and hide the vegies by grating them in and for a sweet treat I would make chocolate cake and put beetroot in it ... That was their favourite!

Rebecca Joanne Mann

I sat my kids down and told them about the 5 a day rule. 5 pieces of fruit and veg a day. I told them to pick 5 that they liked. Then they drew and coloured them, then we talked about the different colour of fruits and veg and how they were good for you. Then they made a chart every night of the fruit and veg they wanted the next day ... They even tell me now if they are behind on their charts. I started my kids on veggies and fruit really early. I don't hide them as I don't want them to be an issue. Fruit and veg are nice when prepared in ways kids would like. A firm fav' in my house are parsnips roasted in honey and carrots with a peanut butter, orange and honey dip and rice cracker with peanut butter and honey on top. The kids also help me cook them!

Richard Taite

Mashing potato with pumpkin, carrot and parsnip and lightly grilling as a patty as aways got results with my kids.

Sharon Edwards

My son is high functioning autistic and has sensory problems, hence a lot of different vegies he will not eat because of how it tastes in his mouth. We get around it by making his favorite meals of either lasagna and spaghetti bolognese. We steam a lot of different vegies; sweet potato, pumpkin, broccoli, cauliflower, carrots, corn, even zucchini, mash them up and add to the pasta sauce ... He doesn't have a clue!

Suzanne Maclachlan

The easiest way to have children eat their vegies is to educate them on healthy eating and variety ... Loving the purple carrots currently available and sweet too! Keep the size of the snacks smallish so your child is hungry for his next meal

Tanya Ormsby

Right from the beginning when they were old enough to eat solids I gave my kids sushi instead of hot chips, I'd be asked "How do u get them to eat that?" My answer "they know no difference!!" Don't impose your likes and dislikes on them, let them try it all!

Tricia Priest Chilcott

I had a Home Ec. teacher once whose kids hated mashed potato so she put pink colouring into it and called it something like 'paradise surprise' and they loved it!

Eat your vegies every single day
and remember
The more colourful the food
The more nutrients in it!

Buttery Sweet Potato with Cinnamon

SERVES 4

- *500g potatoes, peeled and thinly sliced*
- *2 tbs. (30g) butter*
- *1 tbs. (15ml) milk*
- *1 tsp. cinnamon*

Bring 4 cups (1 ltr.) water to the boil in a medium saucepan. Add the sweet potatoes and bring back to the boil. Reduce the heat, cover and simmer for 15 minutes or until soft. Drain. Add remaining ingredients and mash until smooth.

Caramel Carrot Coins

SERVES 4

- *2 large carrots, peeled and sliced*
- *2 tbs. (30g) butter*
- *2 tbs. brown sugar*

Place carrots in a medium saucepan and bring to the boil, reduce heat to a rolling boil and cook for 5 minutes. Drain, add back to the saucepan with butter and sugar and over medium heat cook stirring for 2 minutes. Serve hot.

Corn & Bacon Wraps

SERVES 4

- 4 corn cobs, husks removed
- 4 bacon rashers
- 2 tsp. wholegrain mustard
- 1 tbs. honey

Preheat oven to 170°C. Wrap a bacon rasher around each cob of corn. Mix mustard and honey and brush over the cobs. Wrap the cobs in foil, seal and put on a baking tray. Cook for 15 minutes, then carefully remove tray from oven and open parcels and put back into oven for a further 10 minutes.

Mashed Potatoes

SERVES 4

- 4 potatoes, peeled
- ½ cup (125ml) milk
- 2 tbs. butter
- ¼ tsp. nutmeg

In a saucepan, cover the potatoes with cold water and bring to a boil. Cook for 20 minutes, or until tender. While the spuds are cooking, slowly heat the milk and butter, in a small saucepan over medium heat. When the potatoes are done, drain and add half the hot milk mixture. Mash the potatoes with a handheld potato masher or an electric mixer. Keep adding the hot milk until you reach the proper consistency (which, of course, varies from family-to-family). Season with salt, pepper, and nutmeg.

Optional: For a Garlic Mash; Melt the butter in a separate pan and add 12 cloves of chopped garlic. Cook gently for 1–2 minutes. Add the milk and complete as above. For Parmesan Mash; do as above but mash in ½ cup finely grated Parmesan cheese.

Crispy Potato Wedges

SERVES 4

- 6 medium potatoes, scrubbed
- 2 tbs. (30ml) olive oil
- 1 clove garlic,
- 1 tsp. dried thyme

Preheat oven to 200°C. Cut the potatoes into wedges. Place the oil, garlic and thyme in a mixing bowl. Add the potatoes and toss until well coated. Place the wedges on a baking tray in single layer and bake for 30 minutes or until tender.

Optional: Serve with a light sprinkling of sea salt.

Tip: Place the raw cut potatoes in a bowl of water for about 20 minutes to remove the excess starch. Drain and pat dry.

Peas & Bacon

SERVES 4

Eat your peas — and love them!

- 1½ cups peas
- 2 rashers rindless bacon, diced
- 1 spring onion, finely diced
- ½ cup (125ml) chicken stock

Place peas in a small pot of boiling water and cook for 2–3 minutes. Remove and drain. In the same pot add bacon, cook for 1–2 minutes stirring before adding spring onion. Cook until bacon is browned. Add peas and stock to the pot and return to the boil. Reduce heat and simmer for 2 minutes or until most of the liquid has been absorbed. Serve with a sprinkle of pepper.

Peas & Carrots

SERVES 4

- *2 cups (500ml) carrots, peeled and sliced*
- *½ cup peas*
- *3 tbs. (45g) butter*
- *⅓ cup (40g) cashew nuts, chopped*

In a medium saucepan bring 2 cups (500ml) of water to the boil, add the carrots and cook for 4 minutes. Add peas and cook for a further 1 minute. Drain, return to heat and add butter and cashew nuts. Mix well and serve immediately.

Perfect Rice

SERVES 6

- *1½ cups (275) basmati rice*
- *3 cups (750ml) water*
- *½ tsp. salt*
- *1 bay leaf*

Place the rice in a sieve and rinse under running water until the water runs clear. Place in a saucepan with a tight-fitting lid. Add the water and bring to the boil over a high heat. As soon as the water boils, add the salt and bay leaf. Stir well. Reduce the heat to very low and simmer for 10 minutes, without lifting the lid. Turn off the heat and allow to stand for 2 minutes before lifting the lid. Transfer to a warm serving dish.

Tip: Use saucepans with glass lids as these prevent removing the lid.

Roasted Vegie Sticks

SERVES 4

- *2 carrots, peeled*
- *2 parsnips, peeled*
- *1 tsp. ground cumin*
- *3 tbs. (45ml) olive oil*

Preheat oven to 180°C. Cut carrots into the size of thick chips, 5cm long. Cut the parsnips a little bigger. Lay the 'vegie sticks' onto a paper-lined baking tray and glaze with a mix of cumin and oil. Roast in the oven for 20–25 minutes or until tender. When cooked, place sticks on a paper towel to absorb any excess oil before serving.

Optional: These are also nice using: sweet potato, potato, beetroot, capsicums and zucchinis — just alter cooking times to suit.

Scalloped Potatoes

SERVES 4

These are *goooooood!*

- *600g potatoes, peeled and thinly sliced*
- *⅔ cup (165ml) milk*
- *½ cup (125ml) cream*
- *½ cup (50g) cheddar cheese, grated*

Preheat oven to 180°C. Layer potato slices in a 20cm baking dish, overlapping slightly. Combine milk and cream and pour over potatoes. Sprinkle with cheese, then bake for 45 minutes or until potato is nice and tender and the top golden and bubbling.

Hint: Don't store potatoes near onions because the onions emit gases that cause potatoes to spoil faster.

Sweet Potato Chips

SERVES 4 AS A SIDE DISH

Recipe from the ageless Cyndi O'Meara.

- *1 orange sweet potato, peeled and sliced into 1cm rounds*
- *3 tbs. cold pressed macadamia nut oil*
- *Sea salt*

Preheat oven to 200°C. Place sweet potato in a large baking dish; drizzle with oil, coating well. Bake for 40 minutes or until browned. Sprinkle with sea salt before serving.

Vegetable Shapes

SERVES 2

These put a thrill into eating vegetables!

- *1 potato (200g)*
- *100g piece pumpkin*
- *Olive oil spray*
- *Metal shapes, e.g. stars, hearts, animal shapes etc.*

Slice potato and pumpkin into 2cm thick slices. Cut out as many shapes as possible. Spray with oil and bake in a 180°C oven 15–20 minutes turning halfway through.

Optional: Keep scraps and make a mashed potato and pumpkin on another night.

Zucchini Sticks

SERVES 2–4

- *1 zucchini*
- *1 tbs. olive oil*
- *¼ cup (25g) Parmesan cheese, grated*
- *½ cup (65g) panko breadcrumbs*

Preheat oven to 200°C and line a baking tray with baking paper. Cut the zucchini into slices, 3cm x 1cm, then toss in a bowl with the olive oil. Mix dry ingredients in a plastic bag. Place zucchini, a handful at a time, in the plastic bag, and shake to coat. Bake for 20 minutes. Turn zucchini and bake for another 10–15 minutes or until golden brown.

Hint: Panko is a variety of flaky bread crumb used in Japanese cuisine for a crunchy coating for fried foods. Panko is made from bread without crusts, and it has a crisper, airier texture than most other breadcrumbs. They are available in the Asian section of your supermarket.

What's the strongest Vegetable?

Muscle Sprouts!

The Challenge

Name as many fruit and vegies as you can,
starting with the letters:
A, B, C.

What's 4 Dinner?

Dinner is the perfect time to talk to your kids and listen to what's on their minds. Studies show that kids and teenagers who sit down to family dinners have a significantly lower chance of developing extreme eating behaviours later in life.
Dine as a family. Dinner makes a Difference!

Beef

Bacon & Cheese Patties

SERVES 4

Trust me, your family will *loooove* these!

- *500g lean beef mince*
- *120g bacon, finely diced*
- *1 cup (100g) cheddar cheese, grated*
- *½ cup (140g) BBQ sauce*

Preheat oven to 200°C. In a large bowl, add all ingredients and season with salt and pepper. Mix well before rolling into handfuls and placing on a paper-lined baking tray. Bake for 20–25 minutes or until cooked through. Turn once after 15 minutes.

Optional: Add 1 tbs. freshly chopped parsley to the mix. Parsley is very high in Vitamin C so add it to meals whenever you can.

Beef & Gnocchi Bake

SERVES 4–6

- 500g lean beef mince
- 700g jar of pasta sauce with vegetables
- 300g ready made Gnocchi
- ½ cup (50g) Parmesan cheese, grated

Cook beef mince until browned, breaking up any lumps. Stir in pasta sauce and bring to the boil. Reduce heat and simmer for 5 minutes. Meanwhile cook gnocchi in large saucepan of salted boiling water for 3–4 minutes, drain when cooked. Pour beef mixture into a lasagne dish, top with the gnocchi and sprinkle over Parmesan cheese. Bake for 10 minutes or until the cheese turns golden.

Tip: Season a pot of water after the water boils, as adding salt before takes the water longer to boil.

Beef & Plum Stir-fry

MAKES 4

Kim Bertuzzi says "This is my absolute divine creamy beef stir-fry (without the cream!)

- 500g topside steak, cut into strips
- ½ cup (160g) plum sauce
- 1 cup (170g) raisins
- 1 tbs. English mustard

Place plum sauce and mustard in a pan with ½ cup (125ml) water, bring to the boil and add beef, cook for 8 minutes on high heat. Add the raisins and cook for a further 2 minutes.

Optional: Serve over rice, what could be more simple!

Beef Stroganoff

SERVES 4

This is requested at least weekly.

- *500g beef strips*
- *200g button mushrooms, sliced*
- *1 pkt beef stroganoff seasoning*
- *250g cream cheese*

Heat a non-stick frying pan and lightly brown beef strips. Add mushrooms, sour cream and stroganoff mix, stir well. Add water to achieve your required consistency.

Optional: Serve over rice to soak up the deliciously rich and inviting sauce.

Beef Wraps

SERVES 4

- *¼ cup (65g) whole egg mayonnaise*
- *1 clove garlic, crushed*
- *4 whole-meal wraps*
- *8 slices roast beef*

Combine mayonnaise and garlic in a small bowl then spread over the base of each wrap. Lay two slices of roast beef over the top. Roll up firmly and fold in the ends to enclose the filling.

Optional: Add whatever salad or vegie fillings your kids will eat.

Cottage Pie

SERVES 4

 Margaret Robinson: facebook.com/4ingredientspage

- *500g lean beef mince*
- *500g jar of your favourite pasta sauce*
- *3 potatoes, peeled, cooked and mashed*
- *1 cup (100g) mozzarella cheese, grated*

Preheat oven to 180°C. Brown and cook mince then add the jar of pasta sauce. Reduce heat and simmer for 10 minutes. Transfer to a casserole dish, top with mashed potatoes and sprinkle with cheese. Place in oven and cook for 20 minutes or until the cheese turns golden brown.

Tip: Plan the week's meals with the help of your kids.

Echidna Balls

SERVES 6–8

Recipe from Lisa Kempf.

- *1kg lean beef mince*
- *2 eggs, beaten*
- *1 cup (160g) cooked white rice*
- *2 x 420g cans condensed tomato soup*

Preheat oven to 180°C. Mix mince, eggs and rice together and season. Form into meatballs. Place in a casserole dish and cover with the soup. Cook for 45 minutes. Lisa says "The rice will pop out of the meatballs and is what makes them look like echidnas!"

Economical Meatloaf

MAKES 4

www **Recipe from Karen Yeoman, New Zealand.**

- *400g sausage meat*
- *1 onion, diced*
- *1 cup (130g) breadcrumbs*
- *1 tbs. Vegemite*

Preheat oven 180°C. Mix all ingredients except the vegemite together. Scrape into a paper-lined loaf tin and smooth off the top. Dissolve the vegemite in 1 cup (250ml) boiling water. Pour over meatloaf and bake for 1 hour. Delicious hot or cold the next day in sandwiches.

Mexican Meatballs

SERVES 4

www **Recipe from Nola Henders.**

- *500g lean beef mince*
- *1 egg*
- *1 smallish onion, diced*
- *35g pkt. Taco seasoning mix*

Mix all ingredients together, roll into meatballs and brown in a non-stick frying pan over medium/high heat for 4–6 minutes or until cooked through.

Muffin-Cup Meatloaf

MAKES 12

- *500g lean beef mince*
- *1 egg*
- *2 slices of multi-grain bread*
- *¼ cup (70g) BBQ sauce (plus extra for basting)*

Preheat oven to 180°C. In a large bowl, stir all ingredients until combined. Apportion evenly among the cups of a lightly greased non-stick muffin tray. Baste with a little more BBQ sauce and bake for 30 minutes.

Optional: These are a hit in our home served with mashed potatoes and 'little trees' which is what we Aussies call small florets of broccoli!

Hint: To add vegies, grate in zucchini, onion and carrot or whatever vegies you have in your fridge before baking.

Scrummy Pies

MAKES 12

- *500g lean beef mince*
- *2 cups frozen peas, corn and capsicum, thawed*
- *400g jar of your favourite pasta sauce*
- *4 sheets puff pastry*

Preheat oven to 200°C. In a non-stick frying pan, brown mince, add vegies and season. Pour in sauce and simmer for 10 minutes. Whilst simmering, cut 6 large rounds into each sheet of pastry. Line a non-stick muffin tray with first 12 rounds, spoon in mince mix and top with final rounds of pastry. Seal with a fork. Bake for 20 minutes or until pastry is nice and golden.

Sloppy Joes

Serves 4

Soooo nice!

- *500g lean beef mince*
- *¼ onion, chopped*
- *¼ green capsicum, chopped*
- *¾ cup (185g) ketchup*

In a non-stick frying pan over medium heat, brown the beef, onion, and green pepper and season. Stir in ketchup and mix thoroughly. Reduce heat and simmer for 20 minutes.

Optional: Our boys love this served up on fresh bread rolls as a savoury mince roll.

Taco Bar

Serves 4

- *500g lean beef mince*
- *1 onion, diced*
- *1 pkt. taco seasoning mix*
- *⅔ cup (165ml) cold water*

In a large non-stick frying pan over medium heat, brown the mince with onion; drain fat. Stir in taco seasoning, and cold water. Reduce heat and simmer for 20 minutes. When all your filling ingredients are ready, line them up 'Taco Bar Style' and let your kids make their own custom creations.

Hint: Take advantage of tacos' accommodating nature and make creative use of leftovers as fillings for pies, place mince and cheese between two tortillas to make quesadillas, fry up a flour tortilla shell add lettuce, tomatoes and leftover mince for a 'taco salad' or form into mince patties, add a slice of cheese and a crisp lettuce leaf for 'Taco Burgers.'

Treasure Box

SERVES 4

"Ahoy there me 'arties ... I see treasure ahead!"

- *4 medium potatoes, washed*
- *425g can minced beef*
- *1½ tbs. (25g) butter*
- *75g sweet corn, drained*

Preheat oven to 200°C. Pierce the potatoes all over with a fork, wrap in foil and cook for 45 minutes or until soft. When nearly ready, heat the minced beef in a saucepan until hot. When potato is soft and has cooled a little, slice the top of the potato 80% through. Scoop out the potato and mash it in a bowl with the butter. Fill the shell with the mince. On to four serving plates, dollop the mash. Place the potato on the mash and fill to overflowing with corn. Wedge the lid on top of the yummy 'Treasure Box.'

Optional: The corn resembles gold, you could add diced red and green capsicum for rubies and emeralds!

"When you want something expensive, ask your grandparents."

Matthew, age 12

Poultry

A man decided to start a chicken farm and brought 24 to get started.
A week later he bought another 24 and another 24 the week after that.
When his friend asked how his chicken farm was coming along?
The man replied, "Not one of them has grown yet!
I wonder if I'm planting them too deep???"

Asian Chicken Soup

SERVES 2

- *2 cups (500ml) chicken stock*
- *½ cup (80g) cooked rice*
- *1 large egg, beaten*
- *¾ cup (130g) cooked chicken, shredded*

Stir broth and rice together in a saucepan, bringing to a boil. Add egg and continue to stir until it has cooked. Add the shredded chicken and season with cracked pepper. You may thicken this up a little by using less broth and more rice to make it a 'stew' type dish.

Optional: This recipe is a great way to use any leftover turkey at Thanksgiving and Christmas.

Coconut Encrusted Chicken Fingers

SERVES 4

- *500g chicken tenderloins*
- *200g natural yoghurt*
- *¾ cup (100g) panko breadcrumbs*
- *¾ cup (90g) shredded coconut*

Preheat oven to 180°C. To make this dish easily, create an assembly line: Place chicken strips on one plate. Next to that, place yoghurt in a wide, shallow bowl and combine panko and coconut with a pinch of salt and pepper in another. Take one chicken strip and toss it in the yoghurt. Then gently roll it into the panko/coconut mixture, pressing to coat on each side. Place on a paper-lined baking tray and repeat process until all chicken 'fingers' are on the tray. Bake for 15–20 minutes in the oven or until cooked.

Chicken Macaroni

SERVES 4

Recipe from Kasey Stewart.

- *3 cups cooked macaroni*
- *2 chicken breasts, cooked and shredded*
- *4 rashers rindless bacon, chopped and cooked*
- *400g can condensed tomato soup*

Preheat oven to 180°C. Place macaroni, cooked chicken and bacon in a rectangular baking dish. Pour tomato soup over the top. Place in oven and bake until heated through.

Optional: Sprinkle with grated cheese before baking.

Chicken Pot Pies

MAKES 6

- 420g can condensed cream of chicken soup
- 1 cup (175g) cooked chicken, cubed
- 400g frozen mixed vegies, thawed
- 1 sheet puff pastry

Preheat oven to 180°C. Combine soup, chicken and vegies in a bowl, season with salt and pepper and mix. Set aside. Meanwhile, roll out the puff pastry and using a 7cm biscuit cutter, cut six rounds. Ladle the chicken mixture into six 250ml ovenproof ramekins or dishes. Top with pastry rounds, cut two air vents into the top of each before pinching around the edge to secure. Brush the top with remaining moisture from the chicken mixture to glaze. Bake for 20–25 minutes or until the lid is golden. Allow to cool before serving.

Chicken Spinach Rolls

MAKES 12

Recipe From the Junior Squad of Golf Queensland.

- 400g chicken mince
- 100g pkt baby spinach
- 220g can creamed corn
- 2 sheets shortcrust pastry

Preheat oven to 200°C. Heat a large non-stick frying pan on high, cook mince for 4–5 minutes or until done. When cool, add spinach and corn and season to taste. Halve two sheets of shortcrust pastry, spoon a quarter of the chicken mixture down the long edge of the pastry. Roll to enclose filling and cut into three pieces. Repeat with remaining pastry and chicken mixture. Place rolls on baking paper-lined tray and bake for 30 minutes until browned.

Chicken Schnitzel

SERVES 4

A family favourite from Johnno Petrie.

- *4 chicken schnitzels*
- *3 tbs. (45ml) olive oil*
- *350g jar Napolitano sauce*
- *1 cup (100g) mozzarella cheese, grated*

Heat a non-stick frying pan and add oil. When hot, lightly fry chicken schnitzels. When golden brown on both sides, place on a paper-lined baking tray. Top evenly with Napolitano sauce and cheese and grill slowly until cheese is bubbling and golden.

You Tube *4ingredientschannel/Chicken Schnitzel*

Easy Chicken Stir-fry

SERVES 4

- *600g chicken tenderloins*
- *¼ cup (125ml) salt-reduced soy sauce*
- *3 tbs. honey*
- *1 red capsicum, diced*

Combine chicken, soy and honey and marinate for 15 minutes. Drain chicken but reserve marinade. Over a medium heat, stir-fry chicken in batches until just cooked. Remove from pan and set aside. Add capsicum and lightly cook, then return chicken to pan, add marinade and simmer for 4 minutes.

Optional: Serve with Udon noodles.

Mango Chicken Pops

SERVES 4

- 1½ chicken breasts, sliced into 2cm strips
- ½ cup (125g) mango yoghurt
- 1 cup (100g) cornflakes, crushed
- ½ cup (150g) mango chutney

Preheat oven to 200°C. Thread chicken strips onto a wooden skewer stick (soaked in water for an hour prior to prevent burning). Roll chicken strips in yoghurt then coat with crushed cornflakes. Bake on a baking paper-lined tray for 20 minutes or until done. Serve with mango chutney as a dipper.

Option: Serve with Roasted Vegie Sticks p.71

What do you get if you cross a chicken with a cement mixer?

A bricklayer!

Mexican Enchiladas

MAKES 12

- 1½ cups (260g) roasted chicken, shredded
- 12 tortillas
- 1½ cups (150g) mozzarella cheese, grated
- 350g jar enchilada sauce

Preheat oven to 175°C. Warm tortillas in microwave oven for 30 seconds or until soft. Divide the chicken amongst each of the tortillas, roll up and place into a baking dish seam-side down. Top tortillas with half the cheese. Pour over sauce and top with remaining cheese. Bake for 30 minutes or until the topping is golden and bubbling.

Optional: Add some chopped onion and capsicum to the chicken.

Oodles of Noodles Omelette

SERVES 4–6

- 85g pkt instant chicken noodles
- 1 cup (175g) roast chicken, finely shredded
- 2 eggs, beaten
- 3 tbs. cheddar cheese, grated

Soak the noodles with flavouring in 2 cups (200ml) of boiling water in a medium bowl. Drain well before adding the chicken and eggs. Mix well and pour into a 20cm non-stick frying pan with a heat-resistant handle. Cook over a medium heat for 5 minutes, sprinkle with cheese and place under a hot grill for 2–3 minutes or until golden. Cool before slicing into wedges to serve.

Smokey BBQ Chicken Balls

MAKES 24

Recipe by Cathy Bennett.

- *300g chicken mince*
- *2 tbs. smokey BBQ sauce*
- *4 tbs. finely grated carrot*
- *4 tbs. grated zucchini*

Preheat a non-stick pan. In a small bowl, combine all ingredients together and roll into bite-sized balls. Fry over medium heat until golden on all sides.

Optional: Serve with a little bowl of smooth ricotta or sour cream with a touch of sweet chilli sauce for dipping.

Sticky Drumsticks

MAKES 8

- *3 tbs. maple syrup*
- *3 tbs. soya sauce*
- *2 tsp. sesame oil*
- *8 drumsticks*

Preheat oven to 180°C. Mix maple syrup, soya sauce and sesame oil in a large bowl. Add drumsticks and toss to coat well. Place drumsticks on a paper-lined baking tray and roast for 40 minutes, basting occasionally, or until the chicken is golden.

Tip: If you generally opt for chicken breast because they are lower in fat, remember this; meat found in drumsticks and thighs is a little higher in fat than breast meat but 60% of that fat is the healthier mono and polyunsaturated kind. Leg meat delivers double the zinc of breast meat, satisfying 20% of your recommended daily allowance (RDA).

Tandoori Wings

SERVES 6

- *1kg chicken wings*
- *⅓ cup (80g) yoghurt*
- *⅓ cup (75g) tandoori paste*
- *1 small onion, grated*

Preheat oven to 180°C. Get an adult to help cut the wings into two pieces at joints, discard tips. If using drumsticks, cut slits into the flesh (as this helps cook faster). Combine yoghurt, tandoori paste and onion in a large bowl. Add chicken and toss to coat all over. Cover and refrigerate for at least 3 hours or overnight. Place chicken pieces in a single layer on an oiled wire rack in a baking dish. Roast for about 30 minutes for wings and 50 minutes for drumsticks or until golden brown and cooked through.

Optional: Serve with naan bread, mango chutney and salad for a family feast!

Teriyaki Chicken

SERVES 4

- *¼ cup (60ml) tamari soy sauce*
- *¼ cup (60ml) mirin*
- *2 tbs. sugar*
- *500g chicken breast, cubed*

Place first 3 ingredients with ½ cup (125ml) water into a small saucepan and stir over low heat until sugar dissolves. Bring to the boil, reduce heat, and simmer for 3 minutes. Set aside. In a non-stick frying pan, cook chicken for 3–4 minutes or until evenly browned. Return all of the chicken to the frying pan, add sauce and cover. Cook over medium heat for 20 minutes or until chicken is tender.

Optional: Serve with boiled rice and sprinkled with fresh coriander.

Thai Chicken Balls

MAKES 24

Recipe from Angie Covino.

- *500g chicken mince*
- *¼ cup (60ml) oyster sauce*
- *½ cup (185ml) coconut milk*
- *2 tbs. Gourmet Garden Thai blend herbs*

Preheat oven to 180°C. Combine all ingredients in a large bowl. Place rounded tablespoons of mixture into two 12-cup mini-muffin trays. Bake for about 15–20 minutes. Turn out, and serve hot.

Turkey Burgers

MAKES 6

- *1 small onion, diced*
- *1 apple, coarsely grated*
- *450g turkey mince (or chicken, beef, lamb or pork mince)*
- *1 egg*

Place the onion, apple and turkey mince into a bowl and season. Crack egg into a separate bowl and beat lightly using a fork, then add to mince mixture. Using clean hands, mix it all together, then shape into round, flat patties. Cover the patties in glad wrap and chill in the fridge for 30 minutes before cooking. The patties can then be grilled, pan fried or BBQ.

Optional: Serve on seeded buns with lettuce, cheese and yummy burger relish.

Burger Relish

MAKES 1 CUP

- 4 tomatoes, chopped
- 1 apple, peeled, cored and chopped
- 1 onion, roughly chopped
- ½ cup (125ml) mirin

Pop all ingredients into a non-stick frying pan, season and bring to the boil. Reduce heat and simmer for 12 minutes or until reduced in volume. Blend into a sweet, flavoursome sauce for any burger!

jOkE

Why did the turkey cross the road?

To prove he wasn't chicken!

The Challenge

Laughter is a habit, The more you practice, the easier
it becomes. Write down who makes you laugh
and make a point to hang out with them more ☺

_____

Fish & Seafood

In time of test
Family is best.

Burmese Proverb

Easy Cheesy Fish Fingers

SERVES 4

- *1 tbs. (15ml) olive oil*
- *12 fish fingers*
- *4 tbs. (70g) tomato sauce*
- *¾ cup (75g) cheddar cheese, grated*

Heat the oil in a non-stick frying pan over medium heat and cook fish fingers on both sides until golden in colour. Remove and lay on a paper-lined baking tray. Smear each with tomato sauce and then sprinkle with cheese. Grill until the cheese is bubbling.

Easy Peasy Pan-Fried Whiting

SERVES 4

- *1 tbs. (15ml) olive oil*
- *8 x 75g whiting fillets*
- *1 cup frozen peas*
- *1 tsp. butter*

Heat a non-stick frying pan over medium-high heat, add oil and cook fish for 2 minutes each side, or until cooked through. Bring a saucepan of water to boil, add peas and cook for 2 minutes. Drain the peas, lightly mash, then stir in the butter. To serve, place peas on a plate, top with whiting fillets and lightly salt.

Tip: Seafood is a healthy protein and lower in fat.

Fish Parcels

MAKES 8

- 4 sheets filo pastry
- ⅓ cup (75g) butter, melted
- 250g fresh white fish fillet
- 2 tbs. tomato sauce

Preheat oven to 190°C. Line a baking tray with baking paper. Lay one filo sheet on a clean surface and brush lightly with butter. Fold in half lengthwise and then cut in half crosswise. Cover each piece with a damp paper towel. Repeat with remaining sheets. Cut the fish into eight equal parts. Then working with one filo sheet at a time, brush again with butter, place a piece of fish on the bottom third of the sheet, parallel to the edge. Brush with tomato sauce, fold in the long sides and then roll to enclose the fish. Brush the seam with butter to secure. Arrange seam side down. Repeat with remaining ingredients then bake for 15–20 minutes.

Salmon & Corn Cakes

MAKES 8

- 410g can salmon
- 700g potatoes, boiled and mashed
- 120g can corn
- ¼ cup (65ml) mayonnaise

Preheat oven to 180°C. Mix all ingredients together and season with pepper. Shape into cakes and bake for 20 minutes or until golden.

Tempura Fish Bites

MAKES 16

- *500g fresh white fish fillets*
- *⅓ cup (40g) cornflour*
- *1 egg*
- *½ cup (125ml) peanut oil*

Slice the fish into 16 bites, 2cm x 2cm cubes. Pop cornflour into a medium bowl. Add egg and ⅓ cup (85ml) of *really* cold water and mix until just combined (careful not to overbeat). Allow batter to stand for a few minutes. Heat oil in a large frying pan or wok. Dip the fish bites in the batter and allow excess to drain away. Fry until batter is very lightly browned and fish turns white and is cooked through. It is best to fry in batches, so as not to overcrowd the pan.

Optional: Add 1 tbs. lemon juice to the batter to create yummy "Lemony Fish Bites" and substitute the water for really cold soda water if you have any.

Tuna Bites

MAKES 20

- *220g can tuna in spring water, drained*
- *1 egg*
- *3 whole-meal bread slices, grated*
- *3 stalks fresh parsley, finely chopped*

Preheat oven to 180°C. In a bowl, mix all ingredients well and season. Using a heaped teaspoon, roll mixture into equal-sized balls and place onto a non-stick baking tray. Bake for 15–20 minutes or until golden.

Optional: If a little dry, brush with oil prior to baking. Slices of bread are easier to grate if frozen first.

Tuna Pasta Salad

SERVES 4

Quick, easy and delicious!

- *200g pkt shell pasta*
- *220g can tuna in spring water, drained*
- *220g can peas and corn, drained*
- *4 tbs. Thousand Island Dressing*

Cook pasta according to packet, then drain. Pour into
a salad bowl and cool in the fridge for 30 minutes. Mix pasta
with tuna, peas and corn. Add dressing and toss to coat well.

*Optional: Chop in a little finely diced red capsicum for colour
and crunch.*

Yummy Tuna Bake

SERVES 6

If your kids eat tuna, this is bound to become a favourite.

- *400g pkt egg noodles*
- *410g can tuna*
- *1 cup (100g) cheddar cheese, grated*
- *420g can condensed cream of celery soup*

Preheat oven to 180°C. Cook noodles as directed on the
package, then drain and cool slightly. Pop noodles, tuna,
half the cheese and soup into a bowl, season and mix together.
Pour into a baking dish and sprinkle with remaining cheese.
Bake for 30 minutes or until the cheese is bubbling.

Optional: Add ½ cup peas before baking.

Pasta & Pasta Sauces

Noodles are more convenient than ever.

Not only are they cheap but they are accessible.
Remember, when you are pressed for time, thin pasta cook the fastest.
Choose the most slender: Angel hair, capellini or vermicelli.

5-minute Fettuccine Carbonara

SERVES 4

Recipe from Marie McColl.

- *350g pkt fettucine*
- *4 rashers rindless bacon, chopped*
- *3 eggs, beaten*
- *1 cup (100g) grated Parmesan cheese*

Cook pasta according to packet instructions. Meanwhile in a non-stick frying pan cook the bacon until crisp. Mix together eggs and cheese. Drain pasta and pour into a bowl. Immediately add egg mixture and toss to combine. Add bacon and toss again. Serve at once.

Tip: Add frozen peas to the fettucine in the boiling water and cook together for some nutritious greens at dinner.

Bacon & Pesto Pasta

SERVES 4

- *400g pkt penne pasta*
- *8 rashers rindless bacon, chopped*
- *4 tbs. pesto of choice*
- *200ml crème fraîche*

Cook the pasta according to packet instructions. Meanwhile, chop the bacon into bite-sized pieces. Reserve 2 tbs. of the cooking water in a cup, then drain the pasta and set aside. Fry the bacon in the same pan for 4 minutes or until golden. Tip the pasta and reserved water back into the pan and stir over the heat for 1 minute. Remove pan from the heat, spoon in the pesto and crème fraîche and stir to combine.

Optional: Add some sliced mushrooms and top with freshly shredded basil leaves.

Capsicum and Tomato Sauce

MAKES 1½ CUPS

- *1 tbs. (15ml) olive oil*
- *2 tbs. capsicum pesto*
- *300ml jar passata (pureed and sieved tomatoes)*
- *½ tbs. sugar*

Add olive oil to pan and heat gently. Fry capsicum pesto for 1 minute, stirring constantly. Add passata and sugar and bring to the boil. Reduce heat. Partially cover pan and simmer for 15 minutes or until slightly reduced. Season to taste and serve with lamb kebabs or pasta.

Cheeeesy Raviooooli

SERVES 4

TRY THIS!

- *250g ricotta cheese*
- *30g Parmesan cheese, grated (plus extra for sprinkling)*
- *24 wonton wrappers*
- *450g jar of your favourite pasta sauce*

In a small bowl, mix the ricotta and Parmesan together and season to taste. Fill a small bowl with water to seal the ravioli. Lay the wonton wrappers on a clean surface and scoop 1 teaspoon of filling onto half of each wrapper. Dip your fingertip into the water and gently rub along the outer edge of the wrapper. Fold in half pressing along the edge to seal. Repeat to dampen, fold and seal the remaining ravioli. When finished, carefully slip the ravioli into a saucepan of boiling water and cook for 3 minutes or just until the wrappers are translucent. Meanwhile, heat the pasta sauce. Using a slotted spoon, scoop out the ravioli, shake off excess water, and transfer to individual bowls. Top each serving with warm sauce and extra Parmesan cheese.

Hawaiian Pasta

SERVES 4–6

www Recipe from Val Felschow.

- 350g pkt pasta spirals
- 400g tin pineapple pieces
- 150g ham, sliced and lightly fried
- ½ cup peas

Boil pasta in water according to packet instructions or until just tender. Drain, then mix and return to saucepan, add pineapple, peas and ham. Heat through on a very low heat, and dinner is done!

Perfect Pesto Pasta

SERVES 4

- 250g spaghetti
- 20 small florets of broccoli
- 4 tbs. basil pesto
- 2 tbs. Parmesan cheese, grated

Cook pasta according to packet instructions or until tender. About 4 minutes before the pasta is cooked, add the broccoli and simmer. Drain the pasta and broccoli reserving three tablespoons of cooking water. Return to pan with the water, add pesto and stir well (adding more pesto if needed). Divide the pasta into bowls, sprinkle with Parmesan and serve.

Mac 'n' Cheese

SERVES 4–6

This is an ageless classic ... Kids just *LOVE* it!

- *400g pkt macaroni, cooked and drained*
- *1 cup (100g) cheddar cheese, grated*
- *2 eggs, beaten*
- *500ml cream*

Preheat oven to 160°C. Combine all ingredients, except ¼ cup of cheese, season and mix well. Place in a baking dish and bake for 35–40 minutes or until the sauce thickens.

You Tube 4ingredientschannel/Mac'n'Cheese

Sammy Salmon Pasta

SERVES 2

- *3 broccoli florets, quartered*
- *½ cup (125ml) cream*
- *200g salmon fillet, grilled and broken up into small pieces*
- *½ cup cooked angel hair pasta*

Heat a non-stick frying pan. Add broccoli and ½ cup (125ml) of water and bring to the boil. Cook until tender, then drain. Add cream and gently stir, do not let boil. Stir in salmon and mix until heated through. Add pasta and stir thoroughly.

Tip: To get water boiling faster, heat some of it in a kettle then add it to the saucepan. Crank up the heat and cover the pan while you are bringing water to a boil; use the boiling time to tackle another step in the recipe!

Spaghetti Bolognaise (Spag-bol)

SERVES 4–6

- *500g lean beef mince*
- *250g thin spaghetti*
- *495g jar pasta sauce with roasted vegetables*
- *1 cup (100g) Parmesan cheese, grated*

Pop 2 tbs. water in a frying pan and add mince; cook on medium heat for 6–8 minutes or until all traces of pink are gone. Season then add pasta sauce, stir, lower heat to a simmer and cook for 6 minutes. Meanwhile cook spaghetti according to paket instructions. Drain and divide equal portions among six bowls. Top with mince and Parmesan cheese.

Optional: Pureeing sweet potato, pumpkin, cauliflower and any other vegie you have and adding them to the pasta sauce is a sure-fire way to get your kids to eat vegies.

Spag-Bol Leftover Ideas

Here are a few ideas so when next you make Spag-bol make extra to use in these scrummy dishes. 2 meals out of 1 — LOVE IT!

Baked Spag-Bol

SERVES 6

- *4 cups leftover spag-bol*
- *50g English spinach leaves*
- *1 cup (100g) mozzarella cheese, grated*

Preheat oven to 180°C. Add prepared spag-bol to a casserole dish (18cm x 28cm). Top with spinach and cheese and bake for 25 minutes or until the cheese is golden brown and the contents are warmed through.

Optional: Grate 1 slice of multi-grain bread over the top of the spinach before sprinkling with cheese and baking.

Spag-Bol Cake

SERVES 6

- 2 cups leftover spag-bol
- 2 eggs
- 1 tbs. parsley, finely chopped
- ⅔ cup (65g) Parmesan cheese, grated

Another idea is to loosen up the spag-bol in the microwave for 1–2 minutes if you've had it in the fridge. Then mix in 1–2 eggs and any condiments you have i.e. olives, sundried tomatoes, herbs etc. Place spag into a 22cm round cake tin smoothing with the back of a spoon, top with cheese and bake in a 180°C oven for 20 minutes or until the cheese browns. Remove and cool for 5–10 minutes. Slice and serve with salad or vegies, whatever your kids will eat ...*Yummy!*

Spag-Bol Log

MAKES 2

- 1 sheet puff pastry, just thawed
- 2 tbs. Gourmet Garden Italian herbs
- 1 cup leftover spag-bol
- ½ cup (50g) mozzarella cheese, grated

Onto your sheet of pastry, smear the Italian herbs, top with spag-bol sauce and sprinkle with cheese. Roll up into a big log and slice into 1½ cm thick slices. Place on a paper-lined baking tray and bake in a preheated 180°C oven for 20–25 minutes.

Spag-Bol Potatoes

MAKES 4

- *4 large (1.2kg) sebago potatoes*
- *2 cups spag-bol sauce*
- *1 cup (100g) cheddar cheese, grated*
- *2 tbs. spring onions, finely chopped*

Preheat oven to 180°C. Scrub and rinse potatoes. Pat dry. Pierce each potato 6 times with a fork and wrap in foil. Place on oven rack. Bake for 1 hour 30 minutes or until tender when a skewer is inserted into centre. Transfer to a plate. Stand for 10 minutes. Top with warm leftover spag-bol sauce, a sprinkle of cheese and spring onions.

Tip: Try stuffing capsicums when in season ... they too are delicious!

Vegie Ribbon Pasta

SERVES 4

- *1 zucchini*
- *1 carrot*
- *1 parsnip*
- *400g jar of your favourite pasta sauce*

Wash the vegies and peel the carrot and parsnip. Take a vegie peeler and make ribbons out of each. Bring a medium saucepan of water to the boil. Add the vegie ribbons and boil for 2–3 minutes. Remove and drain. Pop into a large non-stick frying pan and season. Pour in pasta sauce and simmer until warmed through. Serve immediately.

Optional: Serve sprinkled with Parmesan cheese and garnish with fresh basil.

Pork

What is a home without children?
QUIET!

Henry Youngman

Apple, Carrot & Pork Burgers

MAKES 12

- *1 medium carrot, grated*
- *1 medium Granny Smith apple, peeled and grated*
- *500g pork mince*
- *1 egg, lightly beaten*

Place all ingredients into a medium bowl and season to taste. Using your hands, combine mixture well and form into 12 x 1cm thick patties. Place onto a paper-lined baking tray, cover with plastic and refrigerate for 20 minutes (or until ready to cook). In a non-stick frying pan, add patties and cook for 4–5 minutes each side or until cooked through. Drain on a paper towel.

Optional: To serve, toast an English muffin and top one side with lettuce and tomato, add the burger pattie, drizzle with tomato sauce, add muffin top and serve.

Baby BLTs

MAKES 12

 **Becky Butler: facebook.com/4ingredientspage**

- *12 bake-at-home dinner rolls*
- *6 rashers rindless bacon*
- *2 small tomatoes, sliced thinly*
- *¼ an iceberg lettuce, shredded*

Preheat oven to 180°C. Place bread rolls on a tray and cut lengthways without cutting all the way through. Bake for 5 minutes. Meanwhile, cut the bacon in half and cook in a large, non-stick frying pan until crisp. Just before serving, fill the rolls with bacon, lettuce and tomato.

Optional: Brush rolls with mayonnaise or BBQ sauce before filling.

Boston Beans & Sausages

SERVES 6

- *3 rashers rindless bacon, chopped*
- *1 tbs. maple syrup*
- *420g can baked beans*
- *375g pork sausages, cooked*

In a medium saucepan, fry the bacon over a moderate heat for 3 minutes or until nice and crispy. Add the maple syrup and cook for a further minute, stirring regularly. Add the beans, reduce the heat and simmer for 6 minutes. Add the sausages and cook until warmed through.

Cheesy Sausage Balls

SERVES 6

- 500g sausage mince
- 2 cups (200g) cheddar cheese, grated
- ½ cup (115) butter, softened
- 1 cup (175g) plain flour

Preheat oven to 180°C. Place mince in a bowl and roll into approximately 40 balls. Place each ball onto a paper-lined baking tray and bake for 15 minutes. Into a bowl add remaining ingredients and season with sea salt and pepper. Using your hands, mix to combine. Roll out onto a floured surface and roll into a thin pastry. Cut into squares big enough to encase the balls. Enclose each ball in the pastry, pressing firmly to wrap, and place back onto the tray. Cook for a further 10–15 minutes. Serve with tomato or BBQ sauce to dip.

Sausage Hot Pot

SERVES 4–6

- 6–8 sausages (any flavour you like)
- 1 cup frozen mixed vegetables
- 420g can tomatoes with onion and capsicum
- 420g can Borlotti beans, drained and rinsed

Preheat oven to 200°C. In a large non-stick frying pan cook sausages until brown all over. Remove sausages from pan and cook the vegetables and tomatoes for 5 minutes. Return the sausages and add beans and 1¼ cups (300ml) of water. Mix well. Put into a casserole dish, cover and cook in oven for 25 minutes.

Optional: Try adding some bacon, mixed herbs and apple for sweetness. If you don't have Borlotti beans use baked beans instead.

Sausages with Honeyed Mash

SERVES 2

- ½ sweet potato, peeled and quartered
- 2 beef sausages
- 1 tbs. honey
- 1 tbs. butter

Fill a small saucepan with hot water and bring the sweet potato to the boil until soft. While this is boiling, cook sausages over medium/high heat in a frying pan until browned all over and cooked through, then drain. With a fork, mash the honey and butter through the sweet potatoes until it is a nice 'mash' consistency.

Snag Pie

SERVES 6

- 6 thin sausages
- 2 sheets puff pastry, just thawed
- 4 eggs, beaten

Place sausages in a large bowl and cover with boiling water. Leave until cool, then remove, carefully peel away skins and slice. Line a 25cm quiche dish with baking paper, then one of the pastry sheets. Add sausages, then pour over the egg mix (keep the bowl), gently season to taste. Top with remaining sheet of pastry, seal the edges well with a fork, then trim to neaten. Cut two air vents in the middle, brush with egg residue from the bowl and bake for 45 minutes … This is nice served both hot and cold.

Optional: Cut out shapes with trimmed pastry like a star, heart or map of Australia and pop in the centre of the pie prior to baking.

Sticky Ribs

SERVES 4

- ½ cup (140g) BBQ sauce
- ¼ cup (80g) honey
- 2 cloves garlic, crushed
- 900g Aussie pork ribs

Combine first three ingredients and coat the ribs. Place in a baking dish. Cover with foil. Bake, turning twice, for 30 minutes. Uncover. Bake, turning twice, for 30 minutes.

Optional: Serve with shredded red cabbage and shaved apple tossed in lemon juice and olive oil.

You Tube 4ingredientschannel/Sticky Ribs

Stuffed Sausage

SERVES 6

Recipe from Alanah Smith, New Zealand.

- 6 sausages
- ½ cup (50g) grated cheese
- ½ zucchini, grated
- 6 rashers rindless bacon

Preheat oven 180°C. Slice each sausage to make a pocket, careful not to cut through nor cut all the way to the ends. Mix together cheese and zucchini and stuff into the pockets. Wrap each with a piece of bacon. Place on a paper-lined baking tray. Cook for 25 minutes or until the sausages are cooked through and the cheese is golden and bubbly.

Vegetarian

Welcome to the Church of the Holy Cabbage ...
Lettuce Pray ✝

3-Cheese Pizza

MAKES 2

- ½ cup (50g) mozzarella cheese, grated
- 100g feta, crumbled
- ½ cup (50g) Parmesan cheese, grated
- 2 ready-made pizza bases

Preheat oven to 200°C. Divide the three cheeses between each pizza base. Bake for 10–12 minutes or until cheese melts and the bases are crisp. Remove, cool slightly and cut into wedges to serve.

Optional: Top with Guacamole to serve.

Guacamole

MAKES 1 CUP

- 1 avocado, halved, stone removed, peeled
- ¼ small red onion, finely chopped
- 2 tbs. freshly chopped coriander leaves
- 1 tsp. lime juice

Mash the avocado in a bowl. Stir in the onion, coriander and lime juice.

Baked Bean Baskets

MAKES 4

These are great!

- *4 thick slices of hi-fibre bread, crusts removed*
- *420g can baked beans*
- *2 tsp. butter*
- *½ cup (50g) cheddar cheese, grated*

Preheat oven to 220°C. Butter both sides of bread slices and press into four cups of a muffin tray. Bake for 5 minutes or until the bread is crisp and golden. Heat the baked beans in a pan over low heat until just warm. Spoon the baked beans into the bread cup and sprinkle with the grated cheese.

Broccoli & Cheese Soup

SERVES 8

Soup is a universal comfort food for big and little people and this soup can be made in less than 30 minutes.

- *1 medium yellow onion, finely chopped*
- *2 bunches broccoli, trimmed and coarsely chopped*
- *1 ltr. vegetable stock*
- *½ cup (50g) cheddar cheese, grated*

Cook onion, with 2tbs. water in a saucepan over medium heat for 4–5 minutes, or until softened, stirring occasionally. Add broccoli and stock and bring to the boil. Reduce heat and simmer, partially covered for 20 minutes or until broccoli is tender. Puree in batches until smooth. Season if needed and sprinkle with cheese before serving.

Tip: Broccoli is a Superhero of vegetables with loads of vitamins.

Easy Pumpky Risotto

SERVES 4

- *700g butternut pumpkin, peeled, seeded and cut into 2cm cubes*
- *3 cups (750ml) vegetable stock*
- *¾ cup (140g) Arborio rice*
- *½ cup (50g) Parmesan cheese, grated*

In a saucepan, bring the vegetable stock and pumpkin pieces to the boil, reduce heat, cover and simmer for 10 minutes. Add rice and continue to simmer for 20 minutes, stirring regularly, or until the rice is soft and most of the liquid has been absorbed. Stir through half the parmesan cheese and season. Serve sprinkled with remaining cheese.

Mini-Kids-Quiches

SERVES 4

- *8 slices whole-meal bread, crusts removed*
- *4 eggs, lightly beaten*
- *1 cup (100g) cheddar cheese, grated*
- *1 tsp. mixed herbs*

Preheat oven to 200°C. Gently press bread into non-stick muffin cups. Fill each cup evenly with cheese and herbs and a sprinkle of pepper. Pour into each the egg mixture and bake for 15 minutes or until set.

Tip: If your trays are not non-stick you may need to butter the bread first.

Pear & Cheese Quesadillas

SERVES 4

Quesadillas are often filled with a variety of savoury ingredients, but why not try this delicious option, ideal for brunch, lunch or dinner.

- *4 whole-wheat tortillas*
- *2 tbs. honey*
- *1 cup (100g) mozzarella cheese, grated*
- *1 large ripe pear, cored and thinly sliced*

Lay tortillas on a clean, flat surface and drizzle with honey. Heat a large non-stick frying pan on medium. Place 1 tortilla, honey side up, sprinkle with half the cheese and spread with half the pear. Place another tortilla, honey-side down, over the filling and gently press to 'seal.' Gently flip and cook the other side for 2 minutes or until lightly brown. Transfer to a cutting board and slice into quarters. Then repeat with remaining ingredients. To serve, place two wedges on each of the four plates.

Optional: When adding cheese and pear, add some sultanas or raisins too.

Tip: Ripe juicy pears are loaded with dietary fibre. In most fruit like apples, peaches, nectarines and pears a lot of fibre is found in the skin, so where possible leave fruit unpeeled.

Pizzadilla

SERVES 4

- *4 whole-wheat tortillas*
- *⅔ cup fresh spinach, chopped*
- *⅔ cup (70g) mozzarella cheese, grated*
- *1 cup (250g) Napolitana sauce*

Lay two tortillas on a flat surface. Divide spinach and cheese between the two. Top each with remaining tortillas. Place a non-stick frying pan over medium heat. Gently slide 1 pizzadilla into the pan and cook for 2 minutes or until light golden brown. Using a spatula, gently flip and cook for 1–2 minutes longer or until cheese melts. Remove pizzadilla and cut into triangles. Repeat with remaining pizzadilla. Serve with Napolitana sauce for dipping.

Tip: You can wrap and refrigerate leftovers to take to school for lunch.

What kind of pizza does a man who hates salt like?

A pepper-only pizza!!!!

Popeye's Pie

SERVES 4

- 5 eggs
- 1 tbs. (15ml) olive oil
- 150g pkt spinach leaves
- ½ cup (50g) cheddar cheese, grated

Preheat grill to high. Beat eggs in a bowl and lightly season. In a non-stick frying pan heat oil, add spinach and sauté for a couple of minutes to wilt. Add eggs and cook for 8 minutes, uncovered. Sprinkle with cheese and brown under the grill for 1–2 minutes or until the surface is golden and bubbling. Allow to cool slightly before cutting into wedges to serve.

Tip: If using for lunchboxes the next day, cool, wrap and store in the fridge. Leafy green vegetables like spinach contain Omega-3, an important fatty acid known to help improve concentration.

Quick 'n' Easy Pasta Bake

SERVES 4

- 400g pkt cheese tortellini
- 500g jar of your favourite pasta sauce
- ½ cup fresh basil leaves
- 1 cup (100g) mozzarella cheese, grated

Preheat oven to 180°C. Cook tortellini according to packet instructions. Drain. Toss through pasta sauce and basil leaves. Place in a baking dish and top with mozzarella. Bake for 15–20 minutes or until the cheese is golden brown and bubbling.

Savoury Cake

MAKES 10

- 1 pkt 2 minute chicken noodles
- 4 eggs, lightly beaten
- 300g can creamed corn
- 2 tbs. parsley, freshly chopped

Cook noodles (without flavouring) then drain. Combine noodles with flavour sachet and remaining ingredients. Pour into a small 15cm non-stick frying pan and over a medium heat cook until bubbles start to form on the surface. Using a large spatula flip gently and cook the underside until golden. Serve cut into wedges.

Optional: Sprinkle with cheese and place under a grill until golden and bubbling.

Spaghetti Cupcakes

MAKES 12

"These are AWESOME Mum!" Hamilton, 6 — Kim's son.

- 420g tin spaghetti in sauce
- 4 eggs, beaten
- 2 cups (200g) mozzarella cheese, grated
- Spray oil

Preheat oven to 180°C. In a bowl beat eggs, then add 1½ cups cheese and the spaghetti and stir to combine. Lightly grease the muffin tray and evenly distribute the mixture across the cups. Top each with remaining cheese and bake for 15 minutes.

Optional: This is a great easy kids' meal as they can even decorate the tops of their "cupcakes" with sliced olives, mushrooms, ham or capsicum.

You Tube Broadcast Yourself™ 4ingredientschannel/Spaghetti Cupcakes

Vegetable Frittata

SERVES 4–6

A recipe from Jodie Allanson.

- 6 free range eggs
- 100g mixed frozen carrots, peas and corn
- 100g cherry tomatoes
- ½ cup (50g) cheddar cheese, grated

Preheat oven to 200°C. Line a 20cm x 20cm baking tin with baking paper. In a bowl, whisk the eggs together and season with salt and pepper. In a microwave-safe container, heat the frozen vegies in the microwave until just warm. Slice the cherry tomatoes in half. Pour the vegie mix into the lined tin, and put the tomatoes on the top. Pour the egg mixture over (patting down any tomatoes that are above the egg mixture). Sprinkle with cheese and bake in the oven for 25–30 minutes or until brown and firm on the top.

Vegie Burger

MAKES 4

- 300g can chickpeas
- 2 cups mashed sweet potato
- 300g can peas, corn and carrots, drained
- ½ cup coriander, freshly cut

Pulse chickpeas in a food processor until roughly chopped. Transfer to a bowl. Add remaining ingredients. Season and stir or mash until combined. Using a ¼ cup measure, shape into 12 patties and chill for 30 minutes. Cook in a non-stick frying pan over medium heat for 3–4 minutes on each side or until golden.

Vegetable Nachos

SERVES 2

- 1 (42g) whole-meal pita bread, split in hallf
- ½ avocado, chopped
- 1 tomato, chopped
- ¼ cup (30g) cheddar cheese, grated

Preheat oven to 180°C. Cut each pita half into 8 triangles.
Arrange in a single layer on a baking tray. Bake for 5 minutes
or until pita bread is crisp. Set aside on a plate. Put the avocado,
tomato and 2 tbs. of cheese in an ovenproof dish and season.
Push the pita triangles into the mixture and sprinkle with cheese.
Place the dish on a baking tray. Bake for 6–7 minutes or until the
cheese melts.

What was Snow White's brother's name?

Egg White... (Get the yolk???)

What's 4 Dessert?

Vegetables are a must on a diet. I suggest carrot cake, zucchini bread and pumpkin pie.

Jim Davis

Banana Splitzzzz

MAKES 4

- *4 bananas*
- *8 marshmallows*
- *4 scoops creamy vanilla ice-cream*
- *½ cup (140g) chocolate sauce*

Peel and slice bananas in half lengthways. Place one half on each of the four serving plates. Dollop a scoop of ice-cream to the side, wrap remaining banana around ice-cream and dot with marshmallows. Serve drizzled with chocolate sauce.

Ban-Ola

SERVES 1

- *1 medium sized banana, peeled*
- *½ cup berry yoghurt*
- *½ cup (55g) crushed granola*

Dip banana in yoghurt and roll in crushed granola. Place in freezer bag and freeze. This may be eaten without being frozen also.

Tip: If you can't find granola, substitute with your favourite toasted muesli.

Beehive Cake

Serves 8–10

A recipe from Michele Jenkins who said 'I have used this recipe for over 30 years, it's a big favourite!'

- *2 x 300ml tubs cream*
- *1 unfilled sponge (from supermarket) sliced into 6 layers (3 layers per cake)*
- *1 egg*
- *125g dark chocolate, melted*

Beat 300ml of cream until just stiff, add egg and melted chocolate and mix until thick. Place first layer of cake into a tupperware lettuce container then spread cream mixture onto cake and continue process until the mixture and cake is used up. Cover with glad wrap and place in freezer for 24 hours. Take out and tip out assembled cake. Cover with another 300mls of beaten cream. You can decorate with anything you like (I like a flake chocolate or fresh fruit).

There are no seven wonders of the world
in the eyes of a child.

There are SEVEN MILLION.

Walt Streightiff

Cake POPS

MAKES 24

From the CAKE POP QUEEN herself — Mel Roberts!

- *600g chocolate mud cake*
- *375g milk chocolate melts*
- *1pkt. raspberry jelly crystals*

Line two baking trays with baking paper. Crumble the mud cake and icing into a large bowl and then take a teaspoon of mixture and roll firmly into balls. Chill in the freezer for 20 minutes. In a clean, dry bowl, melt milk chocolate in your microwave stirring every 30 seconds until nice and smooth. Spread jelly crystals onto a flat plate. Working one ball at a time, dip into melted chocolate, allow excess to drip back into the bowl, then place onto prepared trays. Pop into freezer for 20 minutes, then remove and let stand for 5 minutes. Roll or dip into crystals to decorate.

Tip: Mel suggested these fabulous options: white, caramel and red velvet mud cakes work just as nicely and they can also be rolled in white, milk or dark chocolate.

Caramel sTARTs

MAKES 12

- *½ cup caramel Top 'n' Fill*
- *12 (60g) petit vol-au-vents*
- *½ cup strawberries, hulled and diced*
- *¼ cup mini marshmallows*

Mix caramel sauce until smooth and pour into vol-au-vents to the top. Decorate with a strawberry piece and mini-marshmallow.

Optional: Remaining caramel can easily be used in ice-creams, sweet pies or drizzled over fresh fruit kebabs.

Caramel Ice-Cream

SERVES 8

Recipe from the lovely Marie McColl.

- *600ml single (pouring) cream*
- *400g can caramel Top 'n' Fill*

Place the cream in a bowl and using electric beaters whisk until soft peaks have formed. Mix the caramel until smooth and then fold into the cream. Pour into a paper-lined loaf tin and cover. Freeze for at least 4 hours or until firm.

Caramello Slice

MAKES 16

 Peta Watters: facebook.com/4ingredientspage

- *250g block 'Caramello' chocolate*
- *½ cup (115g) butter*
- *200g pkt 'Marie' biscuits, coarsely broken*
- *½ tin sweetened condensed milk*

Melt chocolate and butter in microwave oven, stir in condensed milk and biscuits. Press into a slice tin and sprinkle with coconut if desired. Place in fridge to set! YUM!

You Tube *4ingredientschannel/Caramello Slice*

Choc-Apple Turnovers

MAKES 8

Yummy … Yummy … Yummy!

- *2 sheets puffed pasty*
- *8 tbs. Nutella*
- *2 cups stewed apple*
- *2 tbs. icing sugar*

Cut your puffed pastry sheets in quarters. Generously smear Nutella diagonally from one end to the other. Place stewed apple along Nutella. Fold opposite ends over mixture. Bake in preheated 180°C oven for 15–20 minutes. Sprinkle with icing sugar for decoration.

Chocolate-Chip Pancakes

MAKES 4

Our children love these.

- *1 cup (125g) self raising flour*
- *1 egg*
- *1 cup (250ml) milk*
- *½ cup chocolate chips*

Sift flour, add egg and a pinch of salt. Beat gradually adding milk until thick and smooth. Add chocolate chips. Heat non-stick frying pan. Pour desired quantity into frying pan, cook until bubbling on top and then flip.

Choc Mallow Slice

SERVES 8

Recipe from Julie Forato.

- 200g chocolate
- 15 scotch finger biscuits
- 1 cup small coloured marshmallows
- ½ cup (60g) shredded coconut

In a microwave-safe dish, melt chocolate, stirring every 30 seconds. Cool for 5 minutes. Line a loaf tin with baking paper. Break biscuits into smaller pieces (about 6 pieces per biscuit). Mix all ingredients together in a bowl. Scrape the mixture into the loaf tin, and refrigerate for 1 hour. Slice to serve.

Colourful Custard

SERVES 2

Recipe from the beautiful Julie Forato.

- 50g apricots, roughly chopped
- ⅓ cup (80ml) boiling water
- 1 small ripe banana, peeled and sliced
- 1 tbs. custard powder

Place the apricots into a small saucepan, pour over half the water and simmer for 2–3 minutes. In a food processor, blend the apricots and cooking liquid with the banana. Put the custard powder in a small saucepan and mix in a little of the boiling water to make a paste. Pour over the rest of the boiling water and stir briskly over a medium heat until smooth and creamy. Blend the custard together with the apricot and banana puree.

Creamy Rice

SERVES 6

f Jo Edwards: facebook.com/4ingredientspage
"This is the creamiest rice pudding ever,
even if made on skim milk!"

- *2/3 cup (125g) short grain rice*
- *1/3 cup (85g) sugar*
- *1 ltr. milk*
- *2 tbs. (30g) butter*

In a large saucepan bring all the ingredients to the boil. Reduce heat and simmer until the rice has absorbed all of the milk. This will take approximately 1–1½ hours so stir continuously to avoid the rice sticking to the bottom of the pan and burning.

Fruitilicious-cups

MAKES 6

Use seasonal fruits in such a treat for freshness and flavour.

- *3 kiwifruits*
- *½ a watermelon*
- *3 bananas*
- *3 oranges*

Peel and chop each of the fruits into chunks. Layer evenly between six plastic cups. Serve with a plastic fork … *Yummy!*

Tip: Show your kids the many varieties of melons, let them know that in different parts of the world, rockmelon is known as cantaloupe.

Jelly Slice

MAKES 20

Recipe from Linda Kruger. *THANK YOU* this is *AMAZING!*

- *3 pkt raspberry (or any flavour) jelly*
- *3 cups (750ml) boiling water*
- *1 tbs. gelatin*
- *1 cup (250ml) cream*

Combine jelly crystals, water and gelatin and stir until dissolved. Add cream and stir through. Pour in to a slice tray and refrigerate overnight. Cut into slices before serving.

Lime Bombs

MAKES 40

Jan Neale: facebook.com/4ingredientspage

- *4 cups (480g) desiccated coconut*
- *85g pkt lime jelly crystals*
- *400g can condensed milk*

Combine coconut and ¾ pkt jelly crystals. Add the condensed milk and mix well. Roll the mixture between your palms into little balls, before rolling in the remaining jelly crystals. Place on a baking paper-lined tray and chill before serving.

"You can never be too full for dessert"

Kelly age 4

Healthy Yoghurt Pots

SERVES 1

- *200g tub natural yoghurt*
- *3 dried apricots, finely chopped*
- *1 tsp. honey*

Tip the yoghurt into a serving bowl. Sprinkle with apricots and drizzle with honey.

* Optional Fillings: *Add a teaspoon of fresh fruit jam to the yoghurt with a handful of fresh seasonal berries*

Apple and raisins

Muesli with honey

Banana and dates

Stewed apples and a sprinkle of brown sugar

Nutella Fudge Brownies

MAKES 12

We discovered this beauty when cooking for the American book ... We hope you enjoy it as much as we do!

- *½ cup Nutella*
- *1 large egg*
- *5 tbs. plain flour*
- *¼ cup (30g) hazelnuts, chopped*

Preheat oven to 175°C. Line a 12-cup mini-muffin tray with paper liners. Pop the Nutella and egg in a medium bowl and whisk until smooth. Add flour and whisk. Spoon the batter into the prepared muffin trays (about ¾ full) and sprinkle with the chopped hazelnuts. Bake until a pick comes out with wet, gooey crumbs, about 11–12 minutes. Set on a rack to cool completely. Serve immediately or cover and store at room temperature for up to 3 days.

Meringues Made Easy

MAKES 20

- 4 large organic egg whites, at room temperature
- ½ cup (100g) caster sugar
- ½ cup (60g) icing sugar
- 1 tsp. vanilla

Preheat oven to 100°C. Line two baking sheets with baking paper. In a large glass bowl, beat the egg whites with an electric beater until the mixture resembles a fluffy cloud, then add caster sugar, two tablespoons at a time. Beat for 10 seconds between each addition. When ready, the mixture should be thick and glossy. Sift a third of the icing sugar over the mixture, then gently fold it in with a spatula. Continue to sift and fold in the icing sugar a third at a time, careful not to over-mix, the mixture should look smooth and billowy. Using a tablespoon, drop the mixture in rough rounds onto the baking trays. Bake for 1½ hours or until the meringues sound crisp when tapped and are a pale coffee colour. Leave to cool.

Hint: The most important thing to remember when making meringues is that moisture is their greatest enemy. Therefore, don't make meringues on humid or rainy days and avoid making them when doing other cooking.

Muddy Puddles

SERVES 4

- 420g can creamed rice pudding
- 50g dried apricots, chopped
- ¼ cup (45g) sultanas
- ¼ cup grated chocolate

Empty rice pudding into a bowl and stir in apricots and sultanas. Divide across four individual bowls and sprinkle with grated chocolate to make 'muddy puddles.'

Scotch Finger Slice

MAKES 12

Recipe from Ann-Maree Radford.

- *400g condensed milk*
- *½ cup lemon juice; 1 tsp. lemon zest*
- *300ml cream*
- *220g pkt Scotch finger biscuits*

Beat condensed milk and lemon juice. Then beat the cream until just thickened and fold into mixture. Line a rectangular lamington tray with baking paper and lay the biscuits (flat side up) across the base. Pour the mixture over the biscuits and sprinkle with zest. Refigerate overnight before slicing.

Smartie Top Cookies

MAKES 24

Just try and stop at 1 ... or 2!

- *50g pkt Devil's Food Cake Mix*
- *½ cup (115g) butter, melted*
- *2 eggs*
- *50g pkt Smarties*

Preheat oven to 180°C. Mix first 3 ingredients in a bowl until combined. Line two baking trays with baking paper. Then using a tablespoon, roll into equal-sized balls and place onto trays, allow for spreading. Gently press with a fork and top each with 3–4 Smarties. Bake for 10 minutes, remove and allow to cool and harden.

Optional: Substitute Freckles for Smarties.

Strawberry Garden

SERVES 6

Make a statement!

- *500g fresh strawberries*
- *150g dark chocolate (70% cocoa solids if possible)*
- *150g white chocolate*
- *½ cup 100s & 1,000s*

Firstly wash and dry the strawberries (leaving the stalks in place). Gently push a skewer into each but not all the way through. Place dark chocolate in one microwave-safe bowl, and white chocolate in another. Firstly, melt the dark chocolate stirring every 20 seconds until nice and smooth. Dip each strawberry into the chocolate, rotating it slowly. Lift it out and allow the excess to drain back into the bowl. Stand the skewer into a tall glass or vase. Cool slightly before dipping into 100's & 1,000s or another chocolate. Repeat the process until all strawberries are coated. Allow the strawberries to set fully in the refrigerator for an hour.

Optional: Milk chocolate may also be used.

Tip: Strawberries are the only fruit with seeds on the outside. Each berry has about 200 seeds.

I can't believe it, I can't believe I'm here in this real life eating this real food.

Jaxson age 4

Homemade Takeaway

The nicest thing you can wear is a SMILE.

Grandma!

Baked Popcorn Chicken

SERVES 4

Baked popcorn chicken is a healthier menu item as it is lower in saturated fats!

- *500g chicken tenderloins, cut into bite-sized pieces*
- *½ cup (125ml) buttermilk*
- *1 cup (130g) panko breadcrumbs*
- *1 tsp. onion powder*

Marinate the chicken pieces in buttermilk for 20 minutes. Preheat oven to 180°C and line a baking tray with baking paper. Prepare a plate with panko and onion powder on it. Season with pepper. Piece by piece, remove chicken from milk, shake off excess liquid, roll into seasoning and then place on the pre-prepared tray. Continue until all chicken is used. Bake for 15–20 minutes or until golden.

Hint: Experiment with a variety of seasonings and spices, e.g. garlic powder, celery salt, paprika and cajun seasoning. And if you don't have buttermilk available, add 1 tsp. of vinegar to ½ cup of milk to make your own.

You**Tube** *4ingredientschannel/Baked Popcorn Chicken*

Beloved Burgers

Here are some stellar burger suggestions we received from our fabulous family on Facebook.

Carrot & Zucchini Burgers

MAKES 8 MINI OR 4 JUMBO HAMBURGERS

[f] Rebecca Butler: facebook.com/4ingredientspage

- *400g premium mince*
- *1 egg*
- *1 small carrot, grated*
- *1 small zucchini, grated*

Place all ingredients in a bowl and season. Mix well to combine and with clean hands press/roll into 8 patties. Place on a tray and refrigerate for 30 minutes. Heat a non-stick frying pan and over medium-high heat cook the patties, 3–4 minutes each side or until cooked through.

Optional: Serve on a toasted dinner roll with a drizzle of BBQ sauce, lettuce and thinly sliced tomato.

Fruity Lamb Burgers

SERVES 4

[www] Recipe from Jane Griffiths, UK.

- *500g lamb mince*
- *2 slices whole-meal bread, grated*
- *2 tbs. mango chutney*
- *1 tbs. tomato paste*

Mix all ingredients together and form into burgers. Fry the burgers in a non-stick frying pan for 4-5 minutes on each side or until cooked through.

Sweet Honey Burgers

MAKES 4

f **Prue Blake: facebook.com/4ingredientspage**

- *500g premium mince*
- *¼ cup (80g) honey*
- *½ tsp. cinnamon*
- *2 tbs. kecap manis*

Combine the beef mince, honey, cinnamon and kecap manis in a large bowl and mix well. Let the mixture rest in the refrigerator for 1–3 hours to allow the flavours to blend. Shape the mixture into 4 patties and grill each side for 5 minutes or until the meat is fully cooked.

Optional: Serve in toasted burger buns with a pineapple slice on each burger ... With honey and cinnamon in the beef patty and a sweet slice of pineapple on top — how much sweeter can a burger be?

Zingy Burgers

MAKES 8 BURGERS

f **Noeline Wright: facebook.com/4ingredientspage**

- *500g lean mince*
- *1 tbs. Worcestershire sauce*
- *1 tbs. French onion soup mix*
- *½ onion, finely diced*

Combine all ingredients and mix well. Let the mixture rest in the refrigerator for 1 hour to allow the flavours time to blend. Shape the mixture into 4 patties and, in a non-stick frying pan, grill each side for 5–6 minutes or until the meat is fully cooked.

Hint: For a flavour variation use different varieties of soup mixes eg., Mushroom and Spring Onion and Vegetable.

Calamari Crowns

SERVES 6

- *1 tsp. peppercorns and 1 tsp. sea salt*
- *1 cup cornflour*
- *400g fresh calamari rings or calamari tubes cut into rings*
- *1 cup (250ml) peanut oil*

In a dry pan, roast the peppercorns until they become fragrant and begin to crackle, transfer to a mortar along with sea salt and grind until crushed well. Mix salt and pepper into cornflour and roll the calamari in the mixture, shake off any excess. Place oil in a hot wok (or saucepan) and when hot cook the calamari in batches for 1 minute or until cooked. Drain and serve hot.

Hint: Eat before the grown-ups get them ... Yummy!

Chicken Nuggets

SERVES 2

- *2 chicken breasts, cut into bite-sized pieces*
- *1 cup (130g) breadcrumbs*
- *1 cup (260g) mayonnaise*
- *1 tbs. (15g) butter, melted*

Preheat oven to 180°C. Coat chicken with mayonnaise and roll in breadcrumbs. Lay on a baking paper-lined baking tray. Drizzle with a little butter and bake for 20 minutes.

Crisp French Fries

SERVES 4

The 'crispy crunch' will be well worth it!

- *4 large potatoes, washed (do not peel)*
- *1 ltr. peanut oil*
- *1 tbs. sea salt*

Slice the potatoes into 1cm lengths. Turn and slice again to form long, thin, even French Fries. Soak in a large bowl of water for 10 minutes, stirring occasionally. Drain and dry with absorbent paper. Meanwhile, heat oil in a large saucepan over medium heat, 150°C. Add the potato sticks and blanche for 5 minutes. Remove with a skimmer and place on absorbent paper to cool. Reheat the oil to 180°C, add potato sticks again and fry for 4–5 minutes or until golden brown. Remove, drain and serve dusted with sea salt … *D.i.v.i.n.e!*

Chips

SERVES 4

- *500g pkt frozen crinkle-cut chips*
- *1 tsp. onion salt*
- *¼ tsp. paprika*
- *⅓ cup (30g) Parmesan cheese, grated*

Preheat oven to 220°C. Arrange chips on a paper-lined baking tray. Sprinkle with onion salt and paprika and toss to coat. Bake 15–20 minutes or until lightly browned. Sprinkle with Parmesan cheese to serve.

Coconut Rice

SERVES 4

Recipe from Christine Bartlett.

- 1½ cups (245g) long grain rice
- 400ml can conconut milk
- 1 tbs. sultanas

In a large saucepan add rice, coconut milk and sultanas with 1¼ cups (310ml) of water and bring to the boil. Reduce heat to a low simmer, cover and cook for 12 minutes, remove from heat and stand for 5 minutes.

Fried Chicken

SERVES 4

- 8 pieces of chicken
- 2 cups (500ml) buttermilk
- 1 ltr. peanut oil
- 2 cups (350g) plain flour, seasoned with salt and pepper

Place chicken pieces in a bowl and cover with buttermilk. Cover and refrigerate for at least 4 hours or overnight. Remove chicken from buttermilk, shaking off excess. Toss in flour. Then repeat, doing this twice will result in a yummy crispier coating. Preheat oven to 180°C. Heat oil in a deep fryer (or in a deep saucepan). When hot, add 3 pieces at a time and cook for 6–8 minutes or until a nice rich, golden brown. Place on a wire rack over a baking tray. When all the chicken is fried, place in the oven and bake for 10 minutes or until cooked through.

Hint: Peanut oil is considered one of the best oils for frying because it has a very high smoke point. This means the oil can reach higher temperatures than most oils before it begins to smoke. Plus it does not absorb or transfer flavours, so the same oil can be used for different foods without it affecting the taste of the foods.

Garlic Bread

SERVES 4

- *1 French stick, halved*
- *½ cup (115g) butter, softened*
- *2 large cloves garlic, crushed*
- *1 heaped tbs. parsley, freshly chopped*

Preheat oven to 180°C. Slice the bread halves into 2cm pieces. Take a small bowl and combine butter, garlic and parsley, salt and pepper. Spread the mixture onto each slice. Wrap the halves in foil and bake for 10 minutes.

Optional: Serve warm sprinkled with freshly grated Parmesan cheese.

Healthy Fish 'n' Chips

SERVES 4

- *400g firm white fish fillets (pat dry)*
- *1 cup (100g) polenta*
- *2 tbs. cajun spice mix or any other you might prefer*
- *1 egg, beaten*

Preheat oven to 180°C. Cut fish into 1cm strips. Mix the polenta or cornmeal and spices together in a deep plate, and season. One at a time, dip the fish strips into the egg mixture then roll into the polenta mixture until evenly coated. Repeat until all the fish strips are coated. Line a baking tray with baking paper, place the fish on the tray and bake for approximately 8–10 minutes, turning halfway during this time.

Optional: Serve with chips and salad.

Seasoned Flour — Americana

MAKES 2 CUPS

- *2 cups (350g) plain flour*
- *1 tsp. each ground salt and pepper*
- *1 tsp. garlic powder*
- *¼ tsp. paprika*

Mix together and store in an airtight container until needed.

Seasoned Flour — Basic

MAKES 2 CUPS

- *2 cups (350g) plain flour*
- *1 tsp. salt*
- *1 tsp. pepper*

Mix together and store in an airtight container until needed.

Seasoned Flour — Spicy

MAKES 2 CUPS

- *2 cups (350g) plain flour*
- *1 tsp. ground chilli flakes*
- *2½ tsp. Chinese 5 spice*
- *Salt and pepper*

Mix together and store in an airtight container until needed.
This is a sensational coating before frying chicken, duck and fish
(or just about anything…*yummo!*)

Pizza

Pizza is one of the most versatile dishes around. There are literally thousands of combinations of Pizza Toppings. You are limited only by your imagination and your children's taste buds.

Pizza Dough

MAKES 4

- *7g sachet dry yeast*
- *½ tsp. sugar*
- *2 cups (500g) bread flour, plus extra to dust*
- *1 tsp. olive oil*

Dissolve yeast and sugar in 1¼ cups (315ml) of warm water. Stand for 10 minutes, until frothy. Sift flour and 2 tsp. salt onto a clean work surface to form a mound. Make a well and pour in yeast mixture. With clean hands, mix until well combined. Knead for 5 minutes, until smooth and elastic. Roll into a ball. Dust a large bowl with extra flour and place dough into it. Brush with a little oil to prevent a crust forming. Cover with a clean tea towel and stand in a warm place for 2–3 hours, until doubled in size. Divide dough into four portions and roll out to form the base of your yummy pizzas!

Pizza Sauce

MAKES 1½ CUPS

- *400g can peeled tomatoes*
- *2 tbs. (30ml) olive oil*
- *2 tbs. basil, finely chopped*

Process tomatoes in a food processor and blend until smooth. Stir in remaining ingredients along with 1 tsp. salt.

Bacon Pizza

SERVES 1

A recipe from Scotty Griffin, up-and-coming Chef.

- *3 rashers bacon*
- *3 tbs. pizza sauce*
- *1 piece of pita or Lebanese bread*
- *¼ cup (25g) mozzarella cheese, grated*

Finely dice bacon and fry for 2 minutes. Spread pizza sauce on pita bread, sprinkle with bacon and top with mozzarella cheese. Place in a moderate oven under the grill until the cheese browns. To maintain crisp bread, place directly onto oven racks.

BBQ Pizza

SERVES 4

- *¼ quantity of pizza dough*
- *2 tbs. pizza sauce*
- *1 tbs. BBQ sauce*
- *Toppings of choice: cheese, ham, salami, chopped onion, bacon*

Preheat oven to 200°C. Place dough on a lightly floured surface and use hands to flatten. Gently push out dough with fingertips to form a 5mm-thick round with a slightly thicker edge to prevent topping running off. Place on a non-stick pizza tray and prick several times. Starting from the centre and working in a circular motion, spread the sauces over the dough right to the thicker edge. Scatter with toppings and bake for 15–20 minutes or until the base is crisp and mozzarella melts. Scatter over basil. Cut into wedges and serve.

Cheese & Vegie Pizza

MAKES 8

A recipe from Marie McColl.

- *280g snap frozen mixed vegies, thawed*
- *1 sheet shortcrust pastry*
- *150ml cream*
- *1 cup (100g) grated cheddar cheese*

In a non-stick frying pan over medium heat, cook the vegies for 4 minutes, stirring regularly then allow to cool completely. Lay the pastry onto a paper-lined baking tray and prick the base. Blind bake in a 180°C oven for 4 minutes. Mix the cooked vegies with the cream and half the cheese. Spoon over pastry then sprinkle with cheese. Bake for 15 mintues or un til the cheese has melted and is golden in colour.

Hawaiian Pizza

SERVES 4

- *½ cup pizza sauce*
- *10 slices ham*
- *1 can pineapple pieces, drained*
- *2 cups (200g) cheddar cheese, grated*

Preheat oven to 200°C Spread sauce, then pineapples, then ham slices and cheese on pizza crust. Bake for 15 minutes or until cheese is melted.

Pepperoni Pizza

MAKES 4

The World's most popular pizza!

- *1 cup pizza sauce*
- *4 flat pita bread or pizza crust*
- *1 cup pepperoni, sliced*
- *2 cups (200g) mozzarella cheese, shredded*

Preheat oven to 200°C. Spread pizza sauce over pizza crust. Sprinkle with cheese, season and top with scattered pepperoni. Bake directly on the oven rack, for 8–10 minutes or until cheese is melted, bubbling and beginning to brown. Allow to cool for 5 minutes, then slice to serve.

Pizza Pizza

SERVES 4

A recipe from Kim Bertuzzi.

- *4 tortillas*
- *8 tbs. tomato soup*
- *2 cups smoked chicken breast, sliced*
- *1 cup (100g) mozzarella cheese, grated*

Preheat oven to 200°C. Spread tortilla liberally with tomato soup. Spread chicken evenly over tortillas. Bake for 15–20 minutes or until lovely and golden ... *Scrumptious!*

Choc-Strawberry & Mascarpone Pizza

SERVES 4

- ¼ quantity of pizza dough
- ½ cup (165g) Nutella
- 100g ripe strawberries, hulled and sliced
- ⅓ cup mascarpone

Prepare dough per p. 140. Make deep indents in the dough and prick several times so it doesn't rise too much. Bake for 12–15 minutes or until crisp. Remove from oven, and while hot, spread with Nutella, sprinkle with strawberries and dollops of mascarpone.

JOKE

"Here's your Christmas present, a box of your favourite chocolates."

'WOW, Thanks! ... But it's half empty!'

"Well, they're my favourite chocolates too!!!!"

Savoury Subs

SERVES 4

- *2 hotdog buns, halved*
- *220g can spaghetti*
- *50g ham, thinly chopped*
- *½ cup (50g) cheddar cheese, grated*

Preheat oven to 180°C. Line a baking tray with baking paper and place buns, cut side up, on the tray. Top each with equal amounts of spaghetti, ham and cheese. Bake for 10 minutes or until the cheese is golden and bread is crunchy.

* Optional Fillings: *Avocado, bacon and cheese*

                                             Baked beans and cheese

                                             Meatballs, Swiss cheese and pasta sauce

                                             Chicken, asparagus and cheese

Wok-On

SERVES 4

- *8 sausages*
- *250g pkt thick egg noodles*
- *4 tbs. (60ml) tamari sauce*
- *2 tbs. honey*

Preheat oven to 180°C. Squeeze the sausage meat from the skins into a large bowl, then using 'little hands' roll into meatballs. Place on a baking paper-lined baking tray and cook for 10–12 minutes or until golden brown. Boil noodles according to packet instructions. In a small bowl, mix tamari and honey. Drain noodles and pour into a large non-stick wok. Add sausages and sauce and toss thoroughly.

Optional: Add a variety of sliced vegetables for colour and nutrition.

The Challenge

Be they Pizzas, hamburgers, fish 'n' chips, or
fried chicken ... This week try to cook your own
TASTY TAKEAWAY; help Mummy and Daddy
by writing down what you like the best.

Love Your Leftovers

Save time and money by combining already-prepared ingredients from last night's dinner with a few on-hand items to create a fresh new meal tonight.

LAST NIGHT: **Hamburgers**

TONIGHT: **TACOS**
Crumble cooked hamburger patties and warm in the microwave oven. Spoon into warmed taco shells and top with salsa, lettuce and cheese.

LAST NIGHT: **Spaghetti Bolognaise**

TONIGHT: **PASTA BAKE**
Place leftover spaghetti bolognaise into a casserole dish. Top with mozzarella and a sprinkling of Parmesan cheese. Cover with foil and bake in a 180°C oven for 30 minutes or until warmed through. For more SENSATIONAL leftover Spag-bol ideas see: Pastas p.103.

LAST NIGHT: **Chicken Enchiladas**

TONIGHT: **TORTILLA SOUP**
Add leftover chopped vegies, e.g. onions, capsicums to a pot with a little olive oil. Sauté until soft. Add chicken stock, shredded leftover chicken and cook until warmed through. Stir in chopped tomatoes or salsa. Serve topped with baked tortilla strips, sour cream and coriander.

LAST NIGHT: Roast Chicken

TONIGHT: **ROMA CHICKEN**

SERVES 4

A recipe from Katrina Price.

- *½ cooked chicken, remove skin*
- *400ml bottle of your favourite tomato based pasta sauce*
- *1 red capsicum, de-seeded and sliced*
- *2 tbs. sour cream*

Cut up chicken, mix with pasta sauce and capsicum in a non-stick frying pan. Season to taste. Bring to the boil. Reduce heat and simmer for 5 minutes. Just before serving stir in sour cream.

Optional: Serve over rice or penne pasta.

LAST NIGHT: Sausages

TONIGHT: **ITALIAN SAUSAGE RIGATONI**

Cook the rigatoni according to instructions. In a large frying pan, sauté leftover chopped sausages and some thinly cut red capsicum. Fold in a jar of your favourite pasta sauce and heat until warmed through. Mix with drained pasta, or serve piled on top. Sprinkle with a little Parmesan cheese.

LAST NIGHT: Mashed Potato

TONIGHT: **SALMON CAKES**

Mix together a tin of salmon, drained, 1 cup of leftover mashed potato, some mayonnaise and about 12 Jatz crackers crushed. Form into cakes and gently fry until golden.

LAST NIGHT: Rice

TONIGHT: **RICE-BASED QUICHE**

MAKES 1

- *1 free range egg*
- *3 cups long grain rice, cooked and warm*
- *3 tbs. finely grated parmesan cheese*

Preheat oven 170°C. Line a quiche dish with baking paper. In a bowl lightly whisk the egg. Add rice and parmesan and mix to combine. Lightly press the mix into the base of the dish. Bake for 15 minutes or until just starting to turn golden brown. Fold bottom third of a tortilla up. Hold in the centre and pivot around forming a cone. Toss together leftover roast chicken, shredded with 2–3 tbs. mild salsa and stuff into cone. Top with grated cheese and lay on a baking tray. Bake in a 180°C oven for 20 minutes … Yum!

Optional: Fill with your favourite quiche filling. Remember the easy quiche recipe from 4 ingredients cleverly combining just eggs, sour cream and your fillings of choice!

LAST NIGHT: Pasta or Noodles

TONIGHT: **EGG & CHICKEN NOODLE SOUP**

SERVES 2

- 2 cups (500ml) chicken stock
- ½ cup cooked pasta
- 2 free range eggs, beaten
- ¾ cup leftover chicken, shredded

Stir the stock and pasta together in saucepan, bringing to a boil. Add eggs and continue to stir until eggs have cooked. Add the chicken and season with cracked pepper. You may thicken this by using less broth and more rice to make it a 'stew' type dish. Serve with bread and vegies.

Optional: Substitute eggs with creamed corn.

PASTA SALAD

Toss your penne with some zesty Italian dressing, chopped tomatoes and minced basil. Top with fresh mozzerella to serve.

Favourites

I was working away on this manuscript late one night, when the idea dawned on me to include this section. Here are recipes from our previous books that my children request over and over again!

Try them, odds are your kids will love them us much as mine do.

Kim

Sweet

Banana Bread

SERVES 8

Two words ... BAKE IT! It's fantastic!

- *2 large ripe bananas, mashed*
- *½ cup (100g) caster sugar*
- *1 cup (260g) whole egg mayonnaise*
- *2 cups (350g) self raising flour*

Preheat oven 180°C. Line a loaf tin with baking paper. In a medium bowl, add bananas and sugar and stir. Add mayonnaise, sifted flour and a pinch of salt then lightly mix, until combined. Pour into tin and cook for 50–60 minutes or until a skewer, inserted into the middle, comes out clean. Allow to cool for 10 minutes, then turn onto wire rack. Enjoy it warm straight from the oven or lightly grill it and then enjoy with butter melting on top.

 *4ingredientschannel/Banana Bread*

Chocolate Balls

MAKES 32

These are always in our fridge or freezer!

- *250g pkt Arrowroot biscuits, crushed*
- *4 tbs. cocoa*
- *400g can condensed milk*
- *½ cup (60g) desiccated coconut*

Mix crushed biscuit, cocoa and condensed milk together to make a sticky consistency. Using a generous tsp. of mixture, roll into balls and cover in coconut. Chill before serving. These can also be frozen.

Tip: Remove from freezer straight into the lunchbox, by morning tea they are 'just right' to eat.

Chocolate Pudding

SERVES 2

- *2 tbs. custard powder*
- *4 tbs. caster sugar*
- *2 tbs. cocoa*
- *1 cup (250ml) milk*

Place first 3 ingredients into a bowl. Stir in half the milk and mix well. Add remaining milk and stir again. Remove spoon, microwave on high for 1 minute, then stir again. Microwave for 15 seconds or until it rises up around the edge. Remove and stir until the pudding looks thick, brown and smooth. Divide across two bowls, cover with cling wrap and chill until ready to serve.

Cookies & Cream Truffles

MAKES 16

These *WILL NOT* last long … Perhaps it has something to do with the delicious filling coming from the biggest selling biscuit of the 20th century!

- *2 x 150g pkt Oreos biscuits*
- *125g cream cheese, softened*
- *150g milk chocolate*
- *50g white chocolate*

In a food processor, crush cookies. Pour into a large bowl and add cream cheese, mixing together until there are no traces of white. Remove mixture and roll into balls, place on a paper-lined baking tray and refrigerate for 45 minutes. Melt milk chocolate over a pan of simmering water or in the microwave, until smooth and runny. Add chilled ball one at a time and coat in the chocolate. Place onto a Roll balls in chocolate mixture to coat. Refrigerate until set.

Optional: For a 'splash' of colour roll these beauties in blue hundreds and thousands for a boy's party or pink for a girl's party.

You **Tube** *4ingredientschannel/Cookies & Cream Truffles*
Broadcast Yourself™

Honey Joys

MAKES 16

- *3 tbs. (45g) butter*
- *⅓ cup (65g) sugar*
- *1 tbs. honey*
- *4 cups (400g) cornflakes*

Preheat oven to 150°C. Heat butter, sugar and honey in small saucepan till frothy, then remove from heat. Add cornflakes and mix well. Spoon into patty-cake cases and bake for 10 minutes.

Mars Bar Slice

SERVES 6

- 3 Mars bars
- 4 tbs. (60g) butter, plus a little extra for greasing
- 4 cups (320g) rice bubbles

In a microwave-proof dish, melt mars bars and butter for a couple of minutes. Add rice bubbles and mix well. Press into lightly greased tray. Refrigerate and cut into slices when ready to serve.

Optional: Trish Grimes from NZ, suggested to replace Mars Bars with Moro Bars.

Nutella Sandwich

MAKES 3

- 6 x 1cm slices ciabatta bread
- ½ cup nutella

Heat a grill pan over medium-high heat. Grill the bread until toasted, about 2 minutes per side. Spread the Nutella over one piece of toast, top with the second and serve.

Peanut Butter Cookies

MAKES AROUND 20

- *1 cup (260g) crunchy peanut butter*
- *1 cup (220g) brown sugar*
- *1 tsp. cinnamon*
- *1 large egg*

Preheat oven to 180°C. Mix all ingredients into a bowl. Spoon small tablespoon sized balls onto two paper-lined baking trays. Slightly flatten with a fork, crisscross style. Bake for 8–10 minutes, or until a thin crust forms on the cookie. Remove from oven and allow to cool completely; these will harden whilst cooling.

Optional: Our beautiful Office Manager Melinda Dines was having a cuppa one day when she said "These cookies would be lovely with choc-chips in them." SHE WAS RIGHT! Substitute cinnamon for ½ cup chocolate bits … D.i.v.i.n.e.

Vanilla Slice

MAKES 8

A crowd-pleasing recipe from Valerie Savage.

- *220g pkt Lattice biscuits*
- *600ml cream*
- *1 pkt vanilla instant pudding*

Place a layer of biscuits in the bottom of a paper-lined lasagne dish, flat side up. With an electric beater, mix together cream and pudding until thick, pour onto the biscuit base and top with another layer of lattice biscuits.

Optional: Eat as is or top with a delicious passionfruit icing.

Savoury

Chicken Carnival Cones

MAKES 8

A recipe by Isobele Whiting and enjoyed by EVERYONE!

- *8 flour tortillas*
- *2 cups leftover chicken meat, shredded*
- *1 cup (250ml) salsa*
- *100g cheddar cheese, grated*

Fold tortilla in half (if small, fold only the bottom third up) and roll into a cone. Fill bottom of cone with chicken, dollop 2 tsp. salsa before covering with a layer of cheese. Place on a paper-lined baking tray and repeat the process until all ingredients are used. Bake in a 180°C oven for 15 minutes.

You Tube *4ingredientschannel/Chicken Carnival Cones*

Crunchy Chicken Fingers

SERVES 4–6

These are sensational!

- *750g chicken tenderloins*
- *¾ cup (185g) natural yoghurt*
- *2 cups (200g) cornflakes, crushed*
- *1 cup (100g) Parmesan cheese, grated*

Preheat oven to 180°C. Combine cornflakes and cheese together in one bowl, and place yoghurt in another bowl. Coat chicken with yoghurt and then cornflake and cheese mixture. Bake in oven for 20–30 minutes, depending on size of chicken breasts.

Healthy Hotdogs

SERVES 4

- 4 wraps
- 4 organic sausages
- 1 cup (100g) cheddar cheese, grated
- 4 asparagus stalks, woody ends removed

Grill or BBQ sausages. Lay wraps out and sprinkle with cheese. Add chosen asparagus and rollup. Grill in sandwich press before cutting in half to serve.

Optional: Drizzle with BBQ sauce prior to baking.

Tip: Preparing asparagus for this dish and any other is a 'snap'... Just bend the ends of several spears until they split in two naturally; discard the rough end.

Lamb Cutlets Kilpatrick

SERVES 4.

These are really scrummy! Morgan is 7 and asks for these EVERY week!!!

- 16 lamb cutlets
- ½ cup (140g) BBQ sauce (may need a little more)
- 6 bacon rashers, chopped and lightly fried

Grill chops until cooked through. Place on a paper-lined baking tray, and spread sauce evenly over each cutlet. Sprinkle with bacon and pop under a warm grill for a few minutes or until bacon is crispy.

Shepherds Pie

SERVES 8

- 500g lean beef mince
- 250g jar fruit chutney
- 800g potatoes, peeled, boiled and mashed
- ¾ cup (75g) tasty cheese, grated

In a non-stick frying pan brown mince, season and mix through chutney. Pour into a casserole dish, top evenly with mashed potato and sprinkle with grated cheese. Bake in a 180°C oven for 20–30 minutes or until cheese is nice and bubbly.

Optional: Slice a tomato or two over the mince before topping with potato.

Vegie Lasagne

SERVES 6

Thanks to Kimmy Morrison for this terrific and very easy dinner!

- 6 sheets lasagna pasta
- 3 cups (150g) mozzarella cheese, grated
- 1 sweet potato
- 500g jar of vegetable pasta sauce

Preheat oven to 150°C. Peel and slice sweet potato then boil until soft, drain liquid and mash. Line a baking tray with baking paper. Place 2 sheets of lasagna side by side. Lightly cover with a layer of cheese. Spoon over some mashed potato covering cheese. Pour over pasta sauce to cover mashed potato. Repeat layering process until last lasagna sheet has been used and cheese, potato and sauce has been laid over the top of the last sheet. Finish off with ½ cup of cheese. Bake for 35 minutes or until cheese is golden and bubbling.

Optional: Fabulous with salad, chips or even more vegetables.

Parties

Children will soon forget your presents,
But they WILL ALWAYS remember your presence.

Chocolate Crackles

MAKES 24

A quick, easy and truly delicious recipe from the beautiful Melanie Roberts.

- *200g milk chocolate*
- *½ cup (110g) butter*
- *3 cups (240g) coco pops*

In a large saucepan over low/medium heat melt together chocolate and butter. Line two mini-muffin trays with papers. Stir coco pops into the melted mixture, coating thoroughly. Divide among papers and refrigerate for 2 hours.

Cinnamon Crackles

MAKES 12

- *2 cups rice bubbles*
- *125g copha, chopped*
- *½ cup (60g) desiccated coconut*
- *2 tbs. cinnamon sugar*

Heat a small saucepan and melt the copha on a low heat, set aside to cool slightly. Line a mini-muffin tray with papers. In a mixing bowl, combine all dry ingredients and add the copha, stirring until well combined. Spoon mixture into papers and refrigerate until firm. Keep refrigerated.

Chocolate Fruit Jewels

SERVES 8

- *340g pkt milk chocolate melts*
- *250g seedless grapes, washed and dried*
- *½ cup 100's and 1000's*

Cover a shallow baking tray with glad wrap. Place chocolate in a large microwave safe bowl and cook on high until nice and smooth, stirring every 20 seconds. Have your grapes washed and dry in a bowl, and fill a small cup with 100's and 1000's. Using a toothpick, dip each grape completely in chocolate, roll in 100's and 1000's and place on the tray. When they are all done, pop them in the fridge for about 20 minutes or until the chocolate has hardened. Remove toothpicks before serving.

Clever Cupcakes

MAKES 12

f **Cassandra Van Brugel: facebook.com/4ingredients**

- *¾ cup (130g) self raising flour*
- *250ml condensed milk*
- *1 egg*
- *⅓ cup (75g) softened butter*

Preheat oven 180°C. Sift the flour into a bowl and add remaining ingredients, beat with electric mixer for 2 minutes until pale and fluffy. Line a patty cake tin with patty papers. Evenly scoop mixture across each and bake for 12 minutes until light golden brown.

Optional: For more of a vanilla taste, add a teaspoon to the batter.

Dinosaur Eggs

MAKES 24

A quick, easy and *yummmmy* apricot ball!

- *500g pkt dried apricots, finely chopped*
- *400g can condensed milk*
- *2½ cups (300g) desiccated coconut (reserve ½ a cup for rolling)*

Combine all ingredients in a bowl. Wet hands and roll two teaspoons of mixture into a 'dinosaur egg'. Repeat with remaining mixture. Roll balls in remaining coconut and refrigerate or freeze.

Ice-Cream Cake

SERVES 12

- *1 ltr. choc-mint ice-cream, slightly softened*
- *2 x 220g pkts chocolate ripple biscuits, crushed*
- *1 punnet of strawberries, sliced*

Press half the ice-cream into a springform pan to form your first layer (approx. 3 cm thick). Ensure you spread the ice-cream right to the outer edges. Top with a layer of crushed biscuits. Fan the edge with strawberry slices, then press in the remainder of the ice-cream and sprinkle with the rest of the crushed biscuits. Press down a piece of baking paper over the top of the ice-cream cake. Store the cake in the freezer overnight. The following day, release the springform pan and run a spatula or long bladed knife around the edge of the cake. Place your serving plate on the top of the cake and quicly, but gently turn the cake over. Remove the base and decorate with fruit of your choice. Once the cake is made, freeze until required.

Tip: You need to work quickly when making this yummy cake, especially in warmer climates.

Jam Drops

MAKES 40

- *1 cup (230g) butter*
- *½ cup (100g) sugar*
- *2 cups (350g) self-raising flour (reserve 2 tbs. for hands)*
- *½ cup Nutella*

Preheat oven 180°C. Line two baking trays with baking paper. Using electric beaters, cream together butter and sugar until light and fluffy. Fold in flour until well combined. Use lightly floured hands to roll teaspoonfuls of mixture into balls. Place on the prepared trays, about 5cm apart. Use a lightly floured finger to make an indentation in the centre of each ball. Spoon half a tsp. Nutella into the centre of each biscuit. for 15 minutes, swapping trays half way through, or until the biscuits are cooked and light golden. Remove and cool.

Jam Starlets

MAKES 24

- *2 sheets short crust pastry*
- *⅔ cup (200g) strawberry jam*
- *100ml cream, whipped*

Preheat oven to 180°C. Cut 24cm x 6cm stars from the pastry. Place into the moulds of two non-stick patty cake tins. Drop 1 generous tsp. of jam into each and bake for 12–15 minutes or until lightly golden. Allow to cool, then transfer to a serving plate. When ready to serve, dollop with a tsp. of cream.

Kebabs

There is something about the fresh, simplicity of kebabs at kid's parties, they add colour, fun and a healthy sensibility most of the time ... Try these for starters.

Hawaiian Kebab

MAKES 8

- *2 pieces of thick bread, crusts removed and cubed*
- *1 cabanossi, sliced into 1cm rounds*
- *400g pineapple, cut into chunks*
- *100g cheddar cheese, cubed*

On a baking sheet, lightly toast the bread cubes in a 160°C oven for 4 minutes. Thread a plain wooden skewer with one cube of bread, followed by a slice of cabanossi, a wedge of pineapple and cube of cheese. End with another cube of toasted bread. Repeat until all ingredients are gone.

Mixed Fruit Kebab

MAKES 8

Recipe from Carly Nelson

- *1 mango*
- *1 kiwifruit*
- *200g watermelon*
- *200g pineapple*

Cut each piece of fruit into chunks or wedges and then thread them onto a plain wooden skewer.

Satay Chicken Kebabs

MAKES 12

- 3 tbs. peanut butter
- ½ tsp. freshly grated ginger
- 1 cup (250g) natural yoghurt
- 3 chicken breasts, skinned and cubed

Mix together the peanut butter, ginger and yoghurt. Cut chicken into bite sized pieces. Pour the yoghurt mixture over the chicken, cover and refrigerate overnight or for at least 2 hours. Thread chicken onto skewers. Grill and gently cook until browned.

Strawberry Shortcake Kebab

MAKES 8

- 250g fresh, ripe strawberries, hulled and halved
- 16 bite-sized cubes of vanilla cake
- 2 tbs. icing sugar

Thread two pieces each of strawberry and cake onto a skewer. Just before serving, dust with icing sugar.

Meat & Cheese Rolls

- Ham, turkey or salami, sliced
- Cheddar cheese, cubed

Roll a piece of the ham, turkey or salami around a cube of cheese and secure with a toothpick. This is a great way to get kids to eat cheese or meat in a fun way.

Hint: Snip off the sharp end of the toothpick for safety.

Party-Sicles

Are a GREAT way to get some goodness into your kids whilst 'partying-on.' Here are the staff at 4 Ingredient's top 4:

Banana-Yogo Ice Blocks

MAKES 6–8

- 4 medium bananas, peeled
- 500g thick natural Greek yoghurt
- 2 tbs. icing sugar
- Squeeze of lemon juice

Slice bananas into chunks and put into a blender, add remaining ingredients and blend until smooth. Pour into moulds and freeze.

Fruit Salad Pops

MAKES 8

- 125g strawberries
- ¼ small rockmelon
- 1 kiwifruit
- 2 oranges, juiced (enough for ¾ cup)

Chop strawberries, rockmelon and kiwifruit into smallish cubes into a bowl and mix thoroughly. Spoon into popsicle moulds or plastic cups and pour over orange juice. Insert paddle-pop sticks into the centre of each mould and freeze for 4–5 hours. Remove pops from moulds to serve.

Mandy-sicles

SERVES 6

 Janelle McCosker: facebook.com/4ingredientspage

- 1 pkt orange jelly crystals
- 125ml boiling water
- 250ml Aussie mandarin juice

In a heatproof bowl, combine jelly crystals and boiling water then stir until crystals are dissolved. Add Aussie mandarin juice and stir. Pour into 6 ice-block moulds and freeze for approximately 4 hours.

Optional: Substitute mandarin juice for orange juice.

Peach and Orange Popsicles

MAKES 4–8

A recipe from our beautiful 4 Ingredients Office Manager — Melinda Dines.

- 3 ripe peaches or nectarines
- 300ml orange juice
- 1–2 tbs. icing sugar
- 4 tinned fruit salad in natural juice

Remove stone from peaches or nectarines, peel and slice. Put into a blender with orange juice and 1 tablespoon of the icing sugar. Blend until smooth. Taste and add more icing sugar to sweeten (if needed). Spoon in fruit salad to half fill the moulds. Pour in juice to cover the fruit salad. Add the rest of the fruit salad into the moulds and top up with juice. Cover and freeze.

Piglet Tails

MAKES 16

- *1 sheet frozen puff pastry*
- *16 Cheerios*
- *½ cup tomato sauce*

Preheat oven to 180°C. Cut 16 thin strips from the sheet of puff pastry. Wrap each around a cheerio and place on a baking tray. Bake for 10–15 minutes, remove and transfer to a serving plate. Serve with tomato sauce to dip.

Sausage Rolls

MAKES 12

Inspired by the beautiful Melanie Roberts.

- *1 green apple, peeled, grated*
- *500g sausage mince*
- *¾ cup seasoned stuffing mix*
- *2 sheets puff pastry, thawed and halved*

Squeeze the moisture from the apple. Place in a bowl with mince and stuffing mix. Season with salt and pepper. Using your hands, mix well. Divide mince mixture into 4 equal portions. Shape each portion into a 25cm long sausage. Place each sausage along one long side of each pastry sheet. Brush edges of pastry with water and roll up firmly to enclose the filling. Cut each roll into six even pieces. Place, seam-side down, onto an oven tray lined with baking paper. Cook in a hot oven (200°C) for about 25 to 30 minutes or until pastry is golden brown and puffed.

Optional: Serve sausage rolls with tomato sauce or tomato chutney.

Hint: These are even easier done as pinwheels.

Toblerone Slice

MAKES 12

- *1 cup (230g) butter, softened*
- *⅔ (165g) cup caster sugar*
- *2¼ (400g) cups plain flour*
- *200g Toblerone chocolate bar, softened*

Preheat oven to 165°C. Using electric beaters, cream the butter and sugar until soft. Add flour and gently mix until combined. Pat firmly into a paper-lined rectangular baking tray and bake for 20 minutes or until the top turns a light golden brown. Using a spatula or a flat spoon, spread the softened chocolate evenly over the baked base. Cool completely. Using a knife, mark squares so that its easier cut when the bars are set. Refrigerate to set. Once set, cut along the pre-marked lines into squares and serve.

White Chocolate Rocky Road

MAKES 24

Inspired by the beautiful Melanie Roberts.

- *375g white chocolate*
- *½ cup (150g) raspberry chewy lollies, halved*
- *3 tbs. desiccated coconut*
- *100g pkt mini marshmallows*

Line two 12-hole mini muffin pans with paper cases. In a ceramic dish, place the chocolate and melt on high in the microwave oven stirring every 30 seconds until nice and smooth. Let cool slightly, stirring constantly. Stir in remaining ingredients and mix well. Spoon mixture into paper cases. Refrigerate until set.

You Tube *4 IngredientsChannel/Rocky Road*

Party Bag Ideas

It's AMAZING how quickly the cost of filling a party bag escalates when you are buying several 'little' items. Here are a few ideas we thought really clever for a lasting memory. Remember to check out ebay when buying in bulk.

4 Ingredients: OKAAAAY so we are biased, but buy them on sale and have the birthday child sign each on his favourite recipe.

Animals: Buy some cheap animals eg., turtles, dinosaurs, farm animals at your local discount store and pop a lovely little 'Thank you' note around their necks.

Books: For each guest, hand-pick a small paperback or Little Golden Book to suit him or her.

Bubbles: Kids *loooove* bubbles!

Crayons and small pads: It may be just what is required to unleash your child's inner Picasso ☺

Disposable Camera: Expect to pay as little as $7 for a 24-exposure disposable camera.

Fake Tattoos: *Come on Mum* … You know you want one too!

Flashlight & batteries: Something a household never seems to have enough of!

Picture Frame: Take a photo of each child with the birthday boy or girl, print it and pop it in the frame to take home.

Piggy Bank: Give every child a piggy bank and pop their first $1 coin into it.

Plant Seeds: A 'budding' gardener may enjoy a packet of tomato seeds or their first mint plant (very hard to kill, it's a goodie to start with!)

Playdough: A little tub of playdough is fun for everyone.

Tape measure: What little boy doesn't like a tape measure?

Tiaras: Shop around for costume jewellery, as there are plenty of bargains for future princesses.

Water pistols: Fun for both boys and girls.

Great Party Games

*I don't know about you lot, but we have been to soooo many
kid's parties lately where the games have been the same…
Pass the Parcel and Treasure Hunt!
Here are some fresh and forgotten ideas I got when I started to chat
about 'Great Party Games' with my girlfriends. Some are even
as old as us (Mmmm … Not quite so fresh!)*

Egg & Spoon Race

4+ PLAYERS

A race of balance! Arrange all of the children at a start line with
1 egg and a teaspoon each. When you are ready to start the
race, ask them to place the egg onto their spoon and then place
their other arm behind their back. When you say go, the children
will race — as fast as they can without the egg rolling out of the
spoon — to the finish line. If the egg falls, that child goes out.
Whoever crosses the finish line first with their egg still balanced
in their spoon and an arm behind their back wins.

Optional: Hard-boiled eggs are best used for children 5 and under.

Gods & Goddesses

4+ PLAYERS

This game requires fairly mellow music. Give each child a book.
When the music starts, the children walk around the room
balancing the books on their heads. When the music stops, the
children must try to go down on one knee. If their book falls off,
he or she is eliminated. The music starts again and the game
continues. The last child left in the game is the winner.

I went to Mars ...

6+ PLAYERS

The children sit in a circle. The birthday child announces *"I went to Mars and I took a..."* then names any object e.g. my DSI. The next child has to repeat this and add another e.g. I went to Mars and I took a DSI and an apple," The third child will add a new object, always keeping the list in order. The game continues around the circle for as long as possible.

Jump the Broom

4+ PLAYERS

Pop a broom on the ground. Play music as the children skip around in a circle, jumping over the broom. When the music stops, the child jumping over the broom, or the last child to jump the broom, is out. Continue until there is one child left.

Lolly Relay

6+ PLAYERS

Divide the children into two teams and have them form lines. Give the first child in each line a pair of mittens. Give everyone a wrapped lolly. When you say "go", the first player in each line puts on the mittens, unwraps the candy and pops it into their mouth. Then, they quickly take the mittens off and hand them to the second person in line. The second player does the same, and so on down the line. The team that finishes first wins.

Optional: For a healthier twist, use chocolate dipped strawberries, or apple quarters.

Musical Statues

6+ PLAYERS

Have the children move around the room whilst the music is playing. Children are free to dance around until the music stops. Once the music stops, children are to freeze where they are and not move. The child who moves first is out of the game. If all of the children are doing an excellent job of remaining still, restart the music. Eventually children will flinch or move and you will get a winner.

Memory on a Tray

4+ PLAYERS

Place a number of objects on a tray in no particular order while the children are in another room or focusing on a different activity. A variety of shapes and sizes work best. For example, a paper clip, fifty cent piece, balloon, biscuit, envelope, fork, etc. The number of objects included is best dictated by the age of the participants — place more objects for older groups and fewer for younger groups. When the children are ready, set the tray down for less than 60 seconds (again, this is best dictated by the children's ages) and then remove it from the room. The children then write down each of the objects they remember from the tray. Whoever is able to list the most objects accurately wins! It's always fun to bring the tray back in and remind the group what was there.

Please let us know on facebook.com/4ingredientspage which of these games you played and liked the best!

The Challenge

Draw or describe your favourite party games

I'm Thirsty

F.A.M.I.L.Y

Father And Mother I Love You ...

*Wise words to remember as told by a young man
from Bloomingdales to Jaxson on our 1st trip to the USA...*

B1 B2 Smoothie

MAKES 2

- *1 ripe banana, chopped*
- *2 cups blueberries (fresh or frozen)*
- *2 cups plain yoghurt*
- *¼ cup honey*

Put all ingredients into a blender along with ½ cup crushed ice and blend until smooth.

Banana-Moooo Smoothie

SERVES 2

- *2 scoops vanilla ice-cream*
- *1 banana*
- *500ml chocolate milk*

Pop ice-cream and banana in a blender and pour in the milk depending on how thick you want the shake. Blend until smooth and frothy.

Optional: Add 1 tbs. peanut butter to this too.

Coconut Dream Smoothie

SERVES 4

- ½ cup (125ml) coconut milk
- 1¼ cups (300ml) pineapple juice
- ⅔ cup pineapple chunks (fresh or tinned)
- 2 scoops vanilla ice-cream

Put the coconut milk, pineapple juice, ice-cream and pineapple chunks into a blender. Blend until smooth. Pour into tall glasses and serve.

Double-Choc Malted Milkshake

SERVES 4

- ⅓ cup malted milk powder
- ⅓ cup chocolate flavoured topping or sauce
- 1 cup chocolate ice-cream
- 2½ cups (625ml) milk

Place all ingredients into blender and blend until smooth and serve.

Tip: For some crunch, after pouring milk shake into glasses, top with chopped or crushed Maltesers.

Fresh Orange Juice

SERVES 2

- 4 oranges

Lightly roll each orange on the counter before cutting each in half. Juice each half; you may also use a citrus reamer to do this. If you want less pulp, use a hand juicer with a strainer.

Fruity-Tutty Smoothie

SERVES 4

- *1 mango, peeled and chopped*
- *4 large strawberries, hulled*
- *200g honey or vanilla yoghurt*
- *1 cup (250ml) milk*

Place all ingredients into a blender with 10 ice-cubes and blend until 'smooth,' use whatever fruits are in season.

Green Slime

SERVES 1

- *5 lychees with half a cup of syrup (from tin)*
- *15 mint leaves*
- *½ cup pineapple juice*
- *10 ice cubes*

Place all ingredients into a blender, and blend together until the ice is completely crushed.

Mango Magic

SERVES 1

W: Sandy Forster

- *1 mango*
- *1 banana, frozen*
- *1 tbs. coconut*
- *1 orange, peeled*

Pop all ingredients into a blender and blend until smooth.

Mango-Tango

SERVES 4

- 1 mango, peeled and chopped
- 1 cup (250ml) pineapple juice
- 1 cup (250ml) orange juice
- 500g vanilla yoghurt

Place all ingredients into a blender with 10 ice-cubes and blend until 'smooth.'

Tip: When mangoes are in season, why not try freezing some mangoes pieces to make better icy smoothies. Plus you can enjoy these yummy smoothies way past the mango season.

Party Punch

SERVES 12–16

- 4 cups of apple juice
- 4 cups of orange juice
- 4 cups of pineapple juice
- 1.25 litre bottle of ginger ale

Mix the 3 juices together in a punch bowl and place in the refrigerator for up to 3 hours. Prior to serving, mix in the ginger ale with extra ice cubes.

Optional: Drain liquid from a can of mixed fruit and pour the fruit into the punch.

Peach-Berry Delight

SERVES 4

- 2½ cups peach slices (fresh or tinned)
- 200g raspberries (fresh or frozen)
- 250g raspberry yoghurt

Place all ingredients into blender and blend until smooth (strain if you don't like raspberry seeds), pour into glasses and serve.

Pretty Pink Smoothie

SERVES 2

- ¼ cup watermelon, chopped
- 3 big strawberries, washed and hulled
- ½ cup (125ml) apple juice
- ¼ cup natural yoghurt

Combine all ingredients in a blender and blend until smooth.

Strawberry Milkshake

MAKES 4 CUPS

- 250g strawberries, chopped
- 2 cups (500ml) milk
- 1 cup strawberry or vanilla ice-cream
- 1½ tbs. strawberry topping

Put all ingredients in a blender and blend until smooth and frothy.

The Challenge

Water is the liquid of life, it is still the healthiest drink on the planet. It hydrates effectively and is, at least in the developed world, the most affordable thing to drink. Kids should always have access to water
... LOTS OF IT!

Keep a record of how much water you drink evey day for a week.

Handy Home Hints 4 Kids

15 minutes

Studies show that talking and listening to your child for 15 minutes *every single day* may be just enough to open up the lines of communication. Remember, you are your child's first teacher ... *TALK, TALK, TALK!*

Baby oil removes crayon

No need to buy expensive cleaners to remove unwanted crayon artwork from walls — all you need is baby oil! Red crayon may be a little more stubborn, but one wipe is usually all it takes!

Baby wipes

Are great for brightening kids' white leather shoes.

Balloons

Party balloons are easier to blow up if they're submerged in hot water for a few seconds beforehand.

Bandaids

Removing is easy if you soak a piece of cotton wool in baby oil and rub over the tape.

Beach

A trip to the beach or lake is always a fun family activity that's also free.

Bicycle Safety Tip

In case of a bicycle accident, tape a card to the child's handlebars containing name, address and phone number

Boiling Pasta

Add at least 4–5 cups of water to a large pot. One tablespoon of salt should be added to the water after it boils. If the salt is added too soon it can give off an odour, which can affect the taste of the pasta. If it is added immediately before the pasta, the salt may not have enough time to completely dissolve in the water. The salt helps bring out the flavour in the pasta and helps it hold its shape.

Bubblegum in hair

To remove, simply rub some peanut butter onto the gummed hair. You will need to wash the hair afterwards but it helps the gum slide off the hair.

Celebrate

An outdoor festival, take the kids and enjoy the day.

Chewing gum in children's hair

Dab with a cloth soaked with eucalyptus oil, gum should come out without tears.

Children's doonas

Place doonas into king-sized covers and tuck the overlap under the mattress to prevent the doonas slipping off.

Cleaning Toys

Clean stuffed toys with cornflour. Rub in, let it stand awhile and brush out.

Clothing Choice

When small children fuss over the clothes you pick out, lay out three outfits and let him choose what he wants.

Colour

Your plate with at least three colours.

Crayon on walls or washable wallpaper

Spray with WD-40®, then gently wipe, using a paper towel or clean cloth. If the mark is stubborn, sprinkle a little baking soda on a damp sponge and gently rub in a circular motion. If the WD-40® leaves a residue, gently wipe off with a sponge soaked in soapy water; rinse clean; blot dry. Another method is to use a hair dryer — it heats the wax and wipes away instantly. If the color remains, like red usually does, wet a cloth with bleach and wipe.

Cuddles

Life's better with cuddles in it!

Exchange Chores

When children protest over doing chores, offer to exchange one of your chores for his.

Fear of Falling

When children are afraid of falling out of bed, place their old crib mattress on the floor next to the bed.

Flat softdrinks

Rather than throwing them out, freeze and turn into icy poles. Kids love them and they are cheap!

Fruit

Cut fruits in different shapes and let your child create faces before eating it.

Fruit salad

Improve flavour of fruit salads by adding ½ cup lemonade; this will also help keep it fresher longer.

Green hair

Remove the green tinge from your hair, as a result of swimming in chlorinated water, by washing your hair in 5 aspirin tablets dissolved in a third cup of shampoo. Or alternatively, 3 tbs. of vinegar in your shampoo.

Heart

Your heart is a muscle, it needs exercise every day.

Homemade cakes and biscuits

Stay fresh longer by placing a sugar cube in the container when storing them.

Involve

The kids in finding a fun recipe for dinner.

Kids' artwork

If you want to save some of your kids' *precious* artwork, simply roll up the artwork and place inside a paper-towel tube. Label the outside with the child's name and date.

Peanut Butter

Add 1 tbs. of peanut butter to your day for a healthy protein.

Pets

The most important thing you can give your pet is love (Oh yeh … Think they may need some food and water too ☺)

Plan

Your weekly menu together.

Plate

Make a plate filled with the colours of the rainbow.

Pocket Money

Learning how to earn money is great, but keep in mind that losing money is part of the lesson kids go through in order to be more careful in the future.

Popcorn

Eliminate unpopped popcorn duds by keeping your unpopped supply in the freezer.

Promote

'Activity' rather than 'exercise' to kids.

Red Means Danger

Mark the caps of all harmful medicine bottles, etc., with red fingernail polish to teach children that they mean danger.

Saving Children's Drawings

Spray drawings and artwork with hairspray to keep colours from fading and smudging.

Safety Tip

Put a piece of colored tape at a child's level on sliding glass doors to prevent them from walking into the door.

Saved By the Bell

Tie a small bell to the door to signal you that a wandering toddler may be on his way outside.

School lunches

Make more fun by using a cookie cutter to cut sandwiches into shapes!

Slip-Proof Glasses

Put a couple of rubber bands around a child's drinking glass to prevent slipping from small hands.

Snack

On dried fruits and nuts.

Soap for Kids

Put bits of soap in an old stocking and tie the end. Children will find it easier to hold.

Spaghetti

When cooking, add a tsp. of cooking oil or a tsp. of butter to the water in rice, noodles or spaghetti. This will prevent the water from boiling over and strands from sticking together.

Stain removers

Reach for baby wipes anytime you notice something on yours or the kids' clothes — sees it gone in no time. We don't know what is in them, but they work a treat.

Strawberries

Purchase strawberries red all-over. The redder near the hull of the fruit the sweeter.

Stuffed toys

To rid toys and teddies of stale smells, place in a paper bag with some baking soda. Shake the bag for a minute, remove toy, brush off remaining powder and pop them in the sun for a while.

Swallowing Pills

Put children's pills in a spoonful of applesauce to make swallowing easier.

To remove a splinter

From a small child, put a little teething gel around it to numb and soften the skin.

Tie a small bell to any door

Leading out of the house and you'll be able to hear a small child making their escape!

Try

A new fruit or vegetable each week.

Vegetables

Have special nutrients that your heart loves.

Wash hands

Wash little (and big) hands thoroughly before eating, and after going to the toilet or playing with pets.

Watermelon

Are far more inviting cut into chunks and left in a bowl in the fridge (and more accessible).

When giving distasteful medicine to kids

First, run an ice cube over their tongue, this temporarily freezes the taste buds.

When travelling with a baby

Take some bicarbonate of soda with you in a small zip-lock bag. Should your baby be sick, simply sprinkle clothes with the soda. Brush off when dry and odour will have disappeared.

Zippers

To make a zipper slide up and down more smoothly, rub a bar of soap over the teeth.

Biographies

Rachael Bermingham

Rachael Bermingham (nee Moore) was born in Stanthorpe on Queensland's Darling Downs in Australia.

Always adventurous, Rachael was a professional shark feeder for 3 years at Underwater World, a state champion in martial arts, and even did a small stint as a stuntwoman at Warner Brothers Movie World before opening up her own travel agency!

An energetic, dynamic and proud mum to 3 gorgeous little boys (including one-year-old twins), Rachael has written 7 bestselling books in the last 5 years and is regarded as one of Australia's #1 female self-published authors.

Rachael commenced her writing career with 'Read My Lips', her first self-published book, in 2005 (an inspirational book for women on getting clear on what they want in life and strategies on how to achieve their goals - available at *www.RachaelBermingham.com*).

While celebrating Rachael's son's first birthday, Rachael gave Kim a copy of 'Read My Lips' and ultimately ignited the *4 Ingredients* journey.

Together, the 2 friends who first met in Kindergarten went on to write five *4 Ingredients* titles selling almost 4 million copies all over the world including Australia, the USA and the UK and have grown the business beyond the books to a multi-million dollar empire which now includes iApps, cookware, TV shows, and other merchandise.

In addition to writing books and speaking at hundreds of events around the world, Rachael mentors other budding authors; showing them how to write, publish and promote their own bestselling books through her book distribution and educational centre 'Bermingham Books ' *(www.Berminghambooks.com)*.

Rachael loves; 'chillaxing' at home with her 3 beautiful boys, friends and family while soaking up the spectacular sun, surf and sand of Queensland's beautiful Sunshine Coast in Australia.

You can contact Rach by:

Email: info@rachaelbermingham.com or
         Rachael@4ingredients.com.au

   facebook/RachaelBermingham.LIVE

         @RachBermingham

         RachaelBermingham.com

Post: PO Box 1171 Mooloolaba QLD 4557 Australia
Phone: +61 488 480 006

Speaking information, bookings, and information about Rachael's other
books can be found at **www.RachaelBermingham.com**

Happy Cooking!

Kim McCosker

Kim McCosker was born in Stanthorpe and raised there until moving to Mundubbera. Schooled on the Gold Coast, completing a degree in International Finance in 1998, Kim trained with MLC as a Financial Planner completing her Diploma in Financial Planning through Deakin University in 2000. Kim's natural ease with people, her ability to communicate effortlessly and her relaxed confidence served her extremely well as a successful financial adviser and later as the Queensland State Manager of MLC Private Client Services. Kim worked for 7 years in the finance industry before finally resigning to spend the time raising her beautiful boys.

It was during this phase of her life that 4 Ingredients was born. Kim had the idea for some time, but it was at the suggestion of her lifelong friend Rachael Bermingham that they write the book ... And so over a couple of red wines began the wonderful rollercoaster ride 4 Ingredients would go on to become.

Taking a year to compile and cook, *4 Ingredients* (or Kim's fourth child as she lovingly refers to it) was born in March, 2007. From an initial print run of 2,000 that were "never going to sell" Kim and Rachael went on to orchestrate what the trade now refers to simply as: *'An absolute phenomenon!'* Having now sold nearly **4 million copies** of their titles (published in 6 different languages), filmed 2 TV series for the Lifestyle Channel (that have broadcast into 18 countries around the world), produced a very popular *iApp – 4 Ingredients*, released a beautiful Cookware range, and have just returned from a sensational tour of the United States of America.

As well, Kim is very excited to be focusing on her solo-journey, which includes:

- **Baby Bowl:** Will be the new baby bible; it is a collection of simple, nutritious baby recipes and wisdom sourced from loving Mothers and Grandmothers to share with you all.

- **4 Ingredients Christmas:** Will be the easiest Christmas cookbook you have ever owned. It will be the first 4 Ingredients title with full colour pictures of all the festive recipes.

- **Public Speaking:** With her warm and personable nature Kim is a popular addition to any Corporate or Charity function where the attendees have to eat.☺

- **Cooking with Kim:** Is Kim's very own TV Channel on YouTube ... A popular choice if you want to learn how to save time and money in the kitchen cooking with just *4 Ingredients*.

But of all that has been done and accomplished, the most rewarding of all is being a Mum to her three precious boys Morgan 9, Hamilton 6 and Flynn 3. For Kim, *family is the most important thing in the world* and with the loving support of her wonderful husband Glen, is able to juggle the demands of a busy work life around her treasured home life.

Life presents many opportunities, but having the courage and the time to purse them in what is an ever increasingly busy and demanding world is hard. But Kim is living proof that you can achieve whatever you want in life with a great idea and lots and lots of **HARD WORK!**

You can contact Kim by:

Email: info@4ingredients.com.au
Office: +61 (7) 5341 8282
Mobile: +61 (431) 297 923
Address: PO Box 400, Caloundra QLD 4551 Australia

 4 Ingredients Channel

 facebook.com/4ingredientspage

 4ingredients.com.au

@4Ingredients

*Be Fabulous
Be You!*

Bibliography

Books

McCosker, Kim: Bermingham, Rachael. **4 Ingredients.** Simon and Schuster Australia Pty Ltd. Suite19A / Level 1 / 450 - 476 Miller St Cammeray NSW 2062 Australia; 2007.

McCosker, Kim: Bermingham, Rachael. **4 Ingredients 2.** Simon & Schuster Australia Pty Ltd. Suite19A / Level 1 / 450 - 476 Miller St Cammeray NSW 2062 Australia; 2008.

McCosker, Kim: Bermingham, Rachael. **4 Ingredients Fast Fresh & Healthy.** Hay House 18/36 Ralph St, Alexandria NSW 2015 Australia; 2010.

Marks & Spencer. **Kids Party Food.** Marks & Spencer P.L.C. PO Box 3339. Chester CH99 9QS. Copyright ©ACP Magazines Ltd 2010.

Murdoch Books. **I want to be a Chef.** Murdoch Books Australia. Pier 8/9 23 Hickson Road, Millers Point NSW 2000.

Rachael Ray. **Yum-o the Family Cookbook.** Clarkson N. Potter, ab imprint of the Crown Publishing Group, a division of Random House, Inc., New York. 2008.

Ruth Berolzheimer. **Culinary Arts Institute Encyclopedic Cookbook.** Culinary Arts Institute, Chicago USA, 1910

Banbery, Sarah. **Healthy Cooking for your Kids.** Parragon Books Queen Street House 4 Queen Street. Bath BA1 1HE, UK. 2006.

Julien, Ronni Litz. **The Everything Cooking for Kids Cookbook.** Adams Media, a division of F+M Media, Inc. 57 Littlefield, Avon, MA 02322 USA 2010.

Holst, Alison. **Children's Step by Step fun-to-cook book.** Hyndman Publishing.325 Purchas Road RD 2, Amberley NZ 7482.

Wardley, Bridget; More, Judy. **The BIG Book of Recipes for Babies, Toddlers and Children.** Duncan Baird Publishers Ltd. 6th floor, Castle House 75-76 Wells Street. London W1T 3QH. 2004.

Bibliography

Webpages

Free Family Nutrition Education – Its Fun!
http://www.nourishinteractive.com/parents_area/family_kids_nutrition_healthy_eating_tips

Recipes for the Whole Family
http://kidshealth.org/parent/recipes/index.html

Top 10 Superfoods & Their Benefits
http://www.squidoo.com/top_10_superfoods

The Cooking Poem
http://childstoryhour.com/storiesfood1htm.htm

Cooking with Kids
http://www.childrensrecipes.com/

Fabulous Foods
http://kidshealth.org/kid/stay_healthy/index.html

The Healthy Living Pyramid
http://www.nutritionaustralia.org/national/resource/healthy-living-pyramid

Kids Cooking
http://www.kidspot.com.au/best-recipes/Kids-cooking+5.htm

Healthy Living
http://www.kidspot.com.au/familyhealth/subsection+190+Family-Health-Healthy-Living.htm

How to pack a healthy kid's lunchbox
http://www.kidspot.com.au/familyhealth/subsection+190+Family-Health-Healthy-Living.htm

Quick and Easy Kids Meals
http://www.simplygreatmeals.com.au/foodfeatures/15/quick-&-easy-kids-meals

Bibliography

Webpages

10 Minute Meals
http://www.10minutemeals.com.au/

Healthy Hoops for Active Kids
http://www.nutritionaustralia.org/act/news/2011/03

School Principals Share Advice for Parents
http://www.chci.org/education_center/page/school-principals-share-advice-for-parents

Healthy Lunchbox Ideas
http://www.freshforkids.com.au/lunch_box/lunch_box.html

Chipwich
www.chipwich.com

Panko
http://en.wikipedia.org/wiki/Panko

The Bub Hub
http://www.bubhub.com.au

Index of Contents

Happy Cooking!

Notes

Notes

Notes

Notes

For a free monthly 4 ingredient recipe subscribe at www.4ingredients.com.au

Notes

For a free monthly 4 ingredient recipe subscribe at www.4ingredients.com.au

Invitation

Join our Foodie-Family

At *4 Ingredients* we cultivate a family of Busy People all bound together by the desire to create good, healthy, homemade meals quickly, easily and economically.

Our aim is to save us all precious time and money in the kitchen. If this is you too, then we invite you to join our growing family where we share Kitchen wisdom daily.

To all who have contributed a recipe or a household hint to this book we would like to extend our sincerest THANKS, your suggestions were really clever, delicious and very much appreciated.

If you have a favourite recipe and think others would enjoy cooking it, or have a great tip on how to save time and money in the Kitchen, then please join our family at:

 4 Ingredients Channel

 facebook.com/4ingredientspage

 4ingredients.com.au

 @4Ingredients

Thank You

Best Wishes & Happy Cooking

Rachael & Kim

Ingredients

MELVILLE SENIOR HIGH SCHOOL
LIBRARY